NORWAY
FLYING HIGH

WHITE STAR PUBLISHERS

FLYING HIGH NORWAY

PHOTOGRAPHS

Antonio Attini

Text
GRAZIANO CAPPONAGO DEL MONTE

Editorial Director
VALERIA MANFERTO DE FABIANIS

Editorial Coordination
VALENTINA GIAMMARINARO
ALBERTO BERTOLAZZI

Graphic Design
PAOLA PIACCO

Cover
Henningsvær is an enchanting village
in the Lofoten Islands.

Back cover
Tradition is very important in Norway: this is well
illustrated by the wooden houses to be found in
this town along the Skagerrak, near Kristiansand.

1
Aust Agder extends on the coast between
Lyngør and Risør.

2-3
In Norway one frequently finds small farms
surrounded by woodlands. Cultivated fields cover
only a little over 6500 sq. miles (10,000 sq. km).

Contents

4-5
Arendal, the Tyholmen area, bounded by the Nedre and Øvre
Tyolmen canals, is famous for its elegant wooden houses.

6-7
Tromsø, above the Arctic Circle, has 55,000 inhabitants
and is the largest city in northern Norway.

8
The mountains of the Narvik hinterland are almost
6500 ft (2000 m) high.

9
The North Cape is considered (mistakenly) to be
the northernmost point in Europe.

10
By Norwegian standards, these little houses along the coast
between Haugesund and Bergen are far too close together.

11
The Hardangerfjord provides the background
to this view near the Folgefonna glacier.

FLYING HIGH NORWAY

The
author

ANTONIO ATTINI WAS BORN IN TURIN IN 1960 AND HAS PRODUCED MANY PHOTO REPORTS ON EUROPE, AFRICA, ASIA AND AMERICA, WHICH HAVE BEEN PUBLISHED BY THE WORLD'S LEADING TRAVEL MAGAZINES. HE HAS WORKED WITH WHITE STAR PUBLISHERS SINCE 1989, TAKING THE PHOTOGRAPHS FOR NUMEROUS VOLUMES IN THE "COUNTRIES OF THE WORLD," "ALL AMERICA" AND "PLACES AND HISTORY" SERIES, AND CONTRIBUTING TO THE CREATION OF MANY OTHER PRESTIGIOUS WORKS. ATTINI HAS BEEN A MEMBER OF THE KODAK GOLD CIRCLE SINCE 1994, WITH THE STANDARD OF EXCELLENCE. IN RECENT YEARS HE HAS SPECIALIZED IN AERIAL PHOTOGRAPHY, SHOOTING FEATURES FROM THE SKIES OF AMERICA AND EUROPE, AND FOR WHITE STAR HE HAS ALSO WORKED ON SEVERAL BOOKS FOR "THE WORLD FROM THE AIR", "A WORLD OF EMOTIONS" AND "FLYING HIGH" SERIES.

14-15
Egersund is an important port for the ferries to and from Denmark. The fjord is between 330 to 750 ft (100 – 230 m) deep and is ideal for navigation.

16-17
The coastline near Kristiansand, the capital of the county of Vest Agder, offers a panorama of reefs, high rocks overlooking the sea and lighthouses.

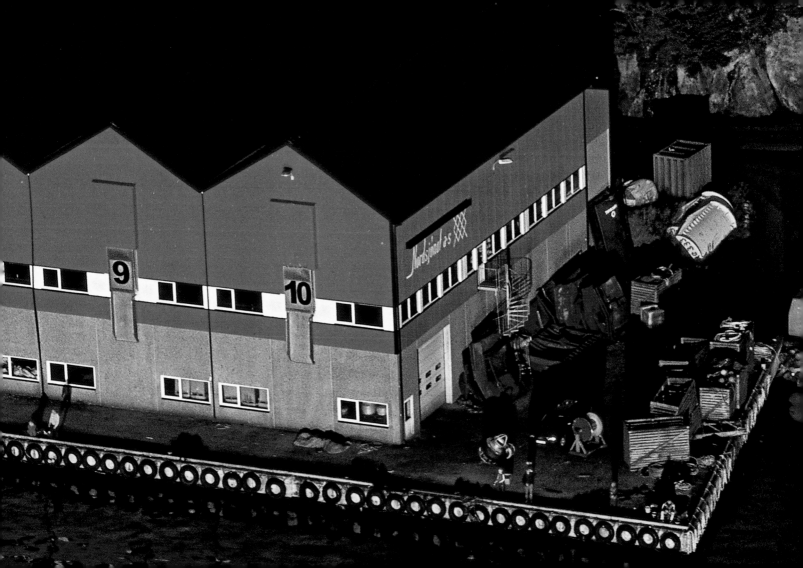

FLYING HIGH NORWAY

Introduction

OF THE THREE SCANDINAVIAN COUNTRIES, NORWAY IS CERTAINLY THE ONE THAT OFFERS THE GREATEST RANGE OF SCENERY. THE SPECTACLE OF THE FJORDS ALONE WOULD MAKE IT UNIQUE, WITH ITS ANCIENT VALLEYS CARVED OUT BY THE RETREATING GLACIERS, WHICH THEN FILLED WITH OCEAN WATER DURING THE THAW THAT SIGNALED THE END OF THE ICE AGE. IN FACT, FROM NORTH TO SOUTH NATURE SHOWS OFF TO THE BEST ALL HER SEDUCTIVE QUALITIES, OFFERING ALWAYS CONTRASTING LANDSCAPES THAT TAKE IN HIGH MOUNTAINS, DRAMATIC ROCK FORMATIONS, DENSE WOODS AND FERTILE PLAINS WHICH CONTRAST WITH THE DESOLATION OF THE RANGING UPLANDS. EVEN THE CLIMATE CAN BE INCREDIBLY MILD IN THE SOUTHERN PART OF THE COUNTRY AND ALONG THE COAST, OR EXTREMELY COLD AND RELENTLESS IN THE NORTHERN INTERIOR AREAS, ALONG THE BORDERS WITH RUSSIA, SWEDEN AND FINLAND.

18
Grimstad is known as the "white city" because of the color
of its houses.

Introduction

AN ENCHANTED COUNTRY, IN MANY WAYS, WHERE THE QUALITY OF LIFE IS EXTREMELY HIGH THANKS TO THE WEALTH DERIVED FROM THE EXPLOITATION OF THE NORTH SEA OIL, THOUGH LET'S NOT FORGET THAT BEFORE THE DISCOVERY OF THIS BLACK GOLD NORWAY WAS BY NO MEANS A RICH COUNTRY. ON THE CONTRARY. UP UNTIL THE MID-20TH CENTURY, MANY FLED FROM HUNGER AND IMMIGRATED TO AMERICA. NORWEGIAN LAST NAMES SPREAD THROUGHOUT THE AMERICAN CONTINENT; PERHAPS THE MOST FAMOUS ONE - IF ONLY FOR A FEW HOURS - WAS THAT OF MARILYN MONROE, WHOSE REAL NAME WAS ACTUALLY MORTENSEN. FISHING AND THE VERY LITTLE FARMING THAT THE CLIMATE ALLOWED PROVIDED THE MAIN MEANS OF SUSTENANCE. THE TRUE WEALTH LAY IN THE MORAL STRENGTH OF A PRACTICAL PEOPLE, ACCUSTOMED TO DEALING WITH THEIR NATURAL SURROUNDINGS BUT WITH A GENTLENESS OF SPIRIT AND, ULTIMATELY, GIVEN OVER TO DREAMS. ONE ONLY HAS TO THINK OF THE EPIC NORDIC TALES, OF THE FAIRY TALES POPULATED BY TROLLS AND GIANTS OR OF THE POPULAR FABLES COLLECTED BY ASBJØRNSEN AND MOE IN THEIR BOOKS.

Introduction

THIS MORAL STRENGTH GAVE RISE TO A HIGH LEVEL OF SOCIALIZATION, A FAR CRY FROM THE TYPICAL BOISTEROUS NATURE OF THE LATIN CULTURE. IT IS ESSENTIALLY PRACTICAL, WITH A SENSE OF SOLIDARITY THAT SHOWS ITSELF IN TIMES OF NEED. A SHINING EXAMPLE IS THAT OF THE FAMOUS EXPLORER ROALD AMUNDSEN WHO, IN THE 1930S, DISAPPEARED IN AN ATTEMPT TO RESCUE THE POLAR EXPEDITION OF UMBERTO NOBILE, CONSIDERED IN FACT A RIVAL IN THE "RACE" FOR THE CONQUEST OF THE POLE. IT THEREFORE COMES AS NO SURPRISE THAT THE COMMITTEE THAT AWARDS THE NOBEL PEACE PRIZE HAS ITS BASE IN OSLO.

ANOTHER TRAIT COMMON TO NORWEGIANS IS THE DEEP BOND THEY FEEL WITH THEIR HOMELAND. FAR FROM BEING CHAUVINISTIC NATIONALISTS, WHEN CALLED UPON THEY KNOW HOW TO BATTLE FIERCELY, AS THEY DEMONSTRATED HEROICALLY AGAINST THE GERMANS WHO OCCUPIED NORWAY DURING THE SECOND WORLD WAR. THE LOVE OF THEIR HOMELAND IS ALREADY EVIDENT IN THE WORDS OF THEIR NATIONAL ANTHEM, "JA, VI ELSKER DETTE LANDET," WHICH TRANSLATES

Introduction

INTO "YES, WE LOVE OUR COUNTRY," AND IS FURTHER CONFIRMED BY THE CARE AND DEVOTION DEDICATED TO THE ENVIRONMENT. OSLO, FOR EXAMPLE, WAS THE FIRST CITY TO INTRODUCE AN ENTRY TOLL; THE CITY ALSO DEVELOPED AN UNDERGROUND ARTERY TO ALLOW PASSAGE FROM EAST TO WEST SO AS NOT TO BLOCK UP ITS CENTER. EVEN THE AIRPORT, WHICH AT ONE TIME WAS LOCATED NEAR THE CITY, HAS NOW BEEN MOVED OVER 25 MILES (40 KM) AWAY. THIS CARE FOR THE ENVIRONMENT IS NOT A PASSING FASHION NOR A PANIC MEASURE, BUT SIMPLY A WAY TO CUT OUT ANY POLLUTION PROBLEMS SINCE THE NORWEGIANS (AS WELL AS THE ENTIRE SCANDINAVIAN POPULATION) ARE PERFECTLY INTEGRATED INTO THEIR SURROUNDINGS. THEY ARE COMPLETELY IN TUNE WITH THEIR ENVIRONMENT: SUN, SNOW, ROCKS, DARK AND DEEP WATERS, WATERFALLS, FORESTS, STEPPE, REINDEER, SALMON, LICHENS, MOSS, FLOWERS, INSECTS. . . . THEY ARE PERFECTLY AWARE OF THE ROLE ASSIGNED TO THEM BY THE CREATOR WITHIN THE MIRACLE OF CREATION AND OF THEIR RESPONSIBILITY AS FAR AS POSSIBLE TO MAINTAIN EVERY-

Introduction

THING EXACTLY AS IT IS. FOR THEMSELVES AS WELL AS THEIR DESCENDANTS.

THE HISTORY AND CULTURE OF NORWAY ARE DEEPLY TIED INTO THOSE OF EUROPE. IN THEIR PURSUIT OF TRADE AND PILLAGE, THE VIKINGS TRAVELED AS FAR AS CONSTANTINOPLE AND SICILY, AS WELL AS ICELAND, GREENLAND AND NORTH AMERICA. ONCE INDEPENDENCE WAS LOST, THE LONG UNION FIRST WITH DENMARK AND SUBSEQUENTLY WITH SWEDEN, INVOLVED NORWAY IN THE AFFAIRS OF THOSE COUNTRIES, EVEN THOUGH ITS STATUS AS A PROVINCE RELEGATED IT TO A SOME-WHAT MARGINAL ROLE. NEVERTHELESS, ARTISTS LIKE IBSEN, HAMSUN, GRIEG, MUNCH AND VIGELAND ARE UNIVERSALLY RECOGNIZED AS SOME OF THE GREATEST ACHIEVERS IN THEIR RESPECTIVE FIELDS.

IN SHORT, NORWAY MIGHT VERY WELL BE CONSIDERED AS ONE OF THE IDEAL PLACES IN WHICH TO LIVE. THE REVERSE OF THE MEDAL, HOW-EVER, IS THAT THOUGH ALWAYS A CHARMINGLY KIND PEOPLE, NORWE-GIANS ARE RESERVED AND SHY, TRAITS THAT CAN BE EXPERIENCED BY SIMPLY ASKING FOR STREET DIRECTIONS; THEY HAVE A CERTAIN

FLYING HIGH NORWAY

24
In early spring the island of Troms is still partly under a white covering.

26-27
The Hardangerfjorden extends from Haugesund to Bergen.

TENDENCY TO ISOLATE AND CLOSE THEMSELVES UP IN THEIR OWN LITTLE WORLD, RELYING ON THEIR OWN STRENGTHS AND NOT WISHING TO DEPEND ON ANYONE. ON TWO OCCASIONS THE NORWEGIANS, ALONE AMONG THE SCANDINAVIAN COUNTRIES, REJECTED A REFERENDUM PROPOSAL TO JOIN THE EUROPEAN UNION. SIGNIFICANTLY ENOUGH, "YES" PREVAILED ONLY IN THE MAJOR (BY THEIR STANDARDS) CITIES: OSLO, BERGEN, TRONDHEIM. . . . THE SMALLER TOWNS AND RURAL COUNTRYSIDE VOTED A MASSIVE "NO," FOR FEAR OF LOSING THEIR LITTLE PRIVILEGES AND THE SUBSIDIES GRANTED BY THE STATE, WHICH WERE INTENDED TO PREVENT DEPOPULATION IN THE MORE RURAL AREAS OF THE COUNTRY.

28-29
Kragerø is one of the most interesting tourist resorts of the southern coast.

30-31
Between the Sørfjord and the Hardangerfjord are several glaciers like this one.

32-33
At one time, the North Cape could only be reached by sea and one had to climb this cliff. Now there is a convenient paved road from Honningsvåg.

LIVING ON
A HUMAN SCALE

FLYING HIGH

FLYING HIGH NORWAY

Of Viking origin, Oslo is the oldest of the Scandinavian capitals. Compared with others, Stockholm or Copenhagen, the Norwegian capital is much less monumental. The reasons for this are rooted in history. Down until 1905, the country had been first a Danish and then a Swedish possession, and Christiania (as Oslo was called from 1624 to 1925) was simply the chief town of a province economically poor but strategically important due to its position as a maritime outpost, as it is demonstrated by the imposing fortress of Akershus. Today it is a city of little more than 500,000 inhabitants, which amounts to about 12 percent of the population of the whole country.

After the peaceful secession from Sweden following a parliamentary resolution, Norway had no need to look for revenge, and its capital very much reflects this sense of tranquility. The architecture is spacious, the buildings never too high, a substantial and majestic city hall with its two uneven lateral towers in dark red brick stands at the bottom end of the fjord, but as for the rest there is nothing particularly heroic. It's really just a peaceful city that snakes along the Karl Johans Gate, the main artery that links the parliamentary building to the large public park in the middle of which rises the royal palace.

Not harboring revengeful motivations does not signify, however, a lesser commitment to beautifying in a worthy fashion the capital of a kingdom. The national heroes have all been given suitable recognition. The theater has been dedicated to playwright Henrik Ibsen; the National Museum has been named after the painter Edvard Munch, and in 1924 the city council set aside for the sculptor Gustav

Living on a Human Scale

Vigeland a large area in which to create freely a sculpture park of statues on the theme of the cycles of life and human relationships. At the end of the path is to be found a grey granite monolith, 56 ft (17 m) high, with 121 figures struggling to reach its summit. Very rarely, in the history of art, has an artist received such full and unconditional support from the institutions and it is due to this that Oslo possesses the Vigeland Parken, one of the most beautiful parks in the world.

Among the Nordic capitals, Oslo is special because of its relaxed atmosphere and high standards of living. This is in part due to the peaceful and kindly nature of the Norwegian people, but also the city's splendid geographical location, between sea and mountains, on a particularly extensive communal area spread over 174 sq. miles (450 sq. km), of which almost 116 (300) have been preserved as green areas; it has a small historic center with many satellite neighborhoods, efficiently linked to the city center and immersed in a natural setting.

In Oslo, great attention is paid to environmental issues, and it could hardly be otherwise in a city that empties itself as soon as an opportunity arises, in summer out to the boats and in winter out on the more than 62 miles (100 km) of community ski slopes. Making things even better were the decisions taken at the end of the last century to move the airport out by approximately 31 miles (50 km) from where it was previously sited close to the city, and also to limit car access to the center by introducing very expensive toll booths and an underground artery for fast through traffic. Around the 1980s, the central area known as the Aker Brygge, a virtually abandoned space containing old naval shipyards and the former railway terminal, was recovered and is now closed to traffic and packed with shops, bars and cultural centers.

Stavanger is the capital of Rogaland, the southwestern part of Norway. It has a population of 100,000 and has been a boom city since the discovery of oil deposits in the North Sea. It is considered the country's oil capital city and it also has a museum that

Living on a Human Scale

illustrates the history of oil and its extraction with models and multimedia reconstructions.

Stavanger is perhaps better known for its "Gamle Stavanger" quarter, an additional UNESCO World Heritage site. This is the historical center of the city, made up of 173 houses built in wood and constituting the largest and best preserved concentration of such houses in Northern Europe. These white-painted houses have been built entirely in wood: frames, walls, floors, ceilings and roofs. The residents of Gamle Stavanger are well aware of their unique location and compete to keep their own homes as polished and well decorated as possible. In other words "*koselig*," an expression not directly translatable that means cozy, likeable and personal. This is a word that conveys an idea of the atmosphere found inside these little homes, surrounded as they are with small gardens and possessing double-glazed windows with little objects or candles displayed for effect between the layers. The houses of this very small area, next to the old port, were until the late 1800s the ex-

clusive homes of wealthy traders. The subsequent economic crisis, the German invasion during the Second World War and other events, all contributed to promoting a newer social mix. Today all sorts of people can be found, including many artists who have converted these homes into galleries.

In statistical terms, Bergen is the rainiest city in Norway, but when the sun at sunset peaks out from behind the clouds, the houses at Bryggen, the old warehouse quarter dating back to the time of the Hanseatic League, of which Bergen was an important city member, light up in a magnificent, colorful spectacle. To the east of Vågen, the old part of the city, lies an area densely packed with small, multi-colored wooden houses, all stacked on top of each other, all with their covered wooden passageways, stairways and alleys. This area occupied by German traders has existed since 1230; it has several times been destroyed by fire but has always faithfully been rebuilt as it was before. The houses acted simultaneously as warehouses or fish shops as well as homes,

FLYING HIGH NORWAY

Tromsø is a small town in continuous expansion, modern and dynamic, located in the northernmost part of the country.

all having essentially the same layout yet each one being unique. Its present appearance dates back to 1702, after the last great fire that destroyed the city. Bryggen, which in 1979 UNESCO designated as a Patrimony of Humanity, is today a highly attractive destination for tourism, with its restaurants, craftsmen shops and studios. Bergen has preserved its long-time vocation for the fishing industry with all its products, and its market is still one of the most important features of the city. Here arrive not only the normal daily catches but also whale meat. "Big men need big food" is a slogan commonly found on the T-shirts on sale in souvenir shops and this trade is strongly supported by the consumers of whale meat, a traditional food in Norway, still hunted and proudly consumed notwithstanding the protests of animal rights activists.

Bergen is surrounded by seven mountain peaks, the highest of which is the Fløyen. Its summit can be reached by cable-car and offers a magnificent view of the city and the fjord, sealed in the distance by a series of small islands. This town is known as the "capital of the fjords" since it is set in the Sogn og Fjordane region, which includes the Sognefjord, the world's deepest and longest fjord.

"Not all ills come to harm us," the old proverb states. This is particularly true for Ålesund. If the terrific fire of 1904 had not destroyed approximately 850 buildings, leaving 10,000 people homeless, they would not have been rebuilt in the Liberty style, known as Jugendstil around there. In the Brosundet area, about 400 buildings were rebuilt inspired by European taste; they constitute, today, the principal attraction of this modest town which extends across

Living on a Human Scale

seven small islets, and effectively render it a museum city. It is sited approximately 155 miles (250 km) above Bergen, north of the fjord region, and is strategically placed to take advantage of the fishing grounds (extended by international agreement to a limit of 200 miles (1610 km) from the coast). They yield largely herring. The city bases its livelihood on fishing; it is from here that the trawlers set out to seek their catch, holds full of cod and herring for foreign markets.

If Oslo is the capital, Trondheim is the historical center and maintains a quite distinctive atmosphere. Its foundation goes back to AD 997, when, under the name of Nidaros, it was the capital of Olav I, Norway's first king, a man who brought Christianity to the country, a feat for which he was canonized. Following his death in battle, Olav was buried at Trondheim, where a church was built modeled along the lines of the great English cathedrals. To emphasize the link with the Norwegian monarchy, the Norwegian Crown Jewels have been brought here and stored in the cathedral. The city has been destroyed repeatedly by fire and only the cathedral remains from its past. Its current set up, with wide boulevards and the Kristian Festung, the fortress King Christian built, dates back to the late 17th century. Fortunately, Trondheim never incurred any direct war damages and everything has remained practically untouched, including its great wooden houses, the famous Stiftsfarden and Singsaker Studenthjem. These are the largest wooden buildings in all of Scandinavia, the former being reserved for the king on his visits to the city, the latter used as a student center. Trondheim has been built at the mouth of a river, the Niver, on the inevitable fjord. The long Trondheimsfjord runs to the northeast-

Living on a Human Scale

southwest and is noted for its characteristic width.

To reach Tromsø by car one has to pass over the 1378 ft (420 m) Mount Storsteiner. Suddenly, rounding a curve, one sees from above the luminous colors of the city, with white and yellow prevailing over the others. Tromsø is located on an island between the mainland and an island farther out; it has a population of 60,000 and it is a young and fashionable city with a notable number of buildings set aside for the large community of university students; the university has the most northerly location in the world and specializes in natural and arctic sciences. The university partially occupies the site of the ancient fishing industry, and where once there had been w arehouses and factories there are now hostels and refectories for the students.

Tromsø has always been an important city, initially as a trading center and later, in the period straddling the 19th and 20th centuries, following the explosion of interest in the race for polar exploration, benefiting from its mid-way position between the polar Arctic Circle and the North Pole by acting as a base for the various expeditions. Today, as a monument to the historical calling, an information center known as Polaris, dedicated to the arctic regions, has been set up. A long, high bridge links the mainland to Tromsø and, just before joining it, one can see the wonderful Arctic Cathedral, a triangular architectural masterpiece, bright and luminous, with its huge 75 ft (23 m) polychrome glass window. At the end of the bridge is the fishing port and then, right beyond, Storgate, the main street which, with its shops and other premises, has earned itself the name of "Paris of the North," as it is referred to by its justly proud inhabitants.

FLYING HIGH NORWAY

45
The Norwegian capital city is built around the Royal Palace, which appears at the center of the photograph.

46

The Karl Johans Gate is Oslo's main artery. At the two ends of this wide, tree-lined avenue lie the Royal Palace and the Parliament building, both visible in the photo.

47 left

The Storting is the Norwegian Parliament. The political system provides for two chambers: the Lagting with 41 members and the Odelsting with124 members, elected for four years by universal suffrage.

47 right

The Spikersuppa is the large park that occupies the center of Karl Johans Gate. For the residents of Oslo, this is a favorite spot in which to take a stroll.

48

The *Rådhuset*, the town hall with its quite unmistakable appearance, was built directly overlooking the port, known as the *Brygge*. The neighboring square is named after the great explorer and Norwegian politician Fritjof Nansen. The yellow building in the background is the university.

49

The Oslo Central Station is located on the continuation of the axis laid down by Karl Johans Gate.

50

The old Red Cross hospital stands out in the heart of Frogner.

51 left

The Havenlageret is a typical building adapted for use as offices between the fortress and the railroad station.

51 right

The Royal Palace is surrounded by a vast park which is open to the public.

52 and 53
The urban layout of Oslo is particularly spacious and the houses are never built right on top of each other.

54

The fortress of Akershus and the castle defended the port area during the Danish domination. The large ferry connects Oslo with Fredrikshamn in Denmark.

55

In this view of the eastern part of Oslo, the ancient military installations and the large white Opera House are clearly visibile.

56
The new Opera House building is an impressive expression of modern architecture and was constructed on the new dock area of the port.

57
Norway boasts a large merchant fleet and Oslo is the main port of the country.

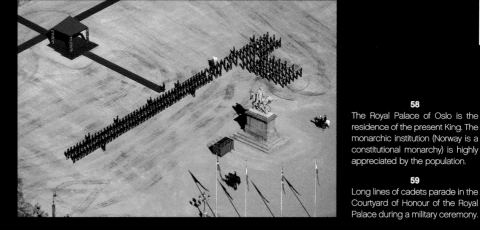

58
The Royal Palace of Oslo is the residence of the present King. The monarchic institution (Norway is a constitutional monarchy) is highly appreciated by the population.

59
Long lines of cadets parade in the Courtyard of Honour of the Royal Palace during a military ceremony.

60

An immense monolith dominates the center of the *Cycle of Life*. The sculptures have been arranged along an axis of about 2,800 ft (850 m) and are divided into five main sections.

61

The Vigeland Parken is named after the sculptor Gustav Vigeland. A short distance farther, and without having to change direction, is the entrance to the cemetery.

62

The statues of this fountain in the shape of trees distinctly resemble
the real trees in the park and recount the various phases of the human life cycle.

63

The granite monolith that concludes the *Cycle of Life* is 55 ft (17 m)
high and has been carved with 121 intertwined human figures.

64-65

The ski jump ramp at Holmenkollen, one of the temples of this sport. Watching these competitions is a "duty" for the inhabitants of Oslo.

66-67

The *stavkirke* of Gol, near Oslo, are very old churches built entirely of wood and are typical of the central southern part of Norway.

68
Many people regularly use boats to reach the city center.

69 left
The shores of the fjord are a much sought-after green zone and a destination for many excursions.

69 right
More boats than cars circulate in Oslo.

70

The lighthouse at Lyngør rises right next to the capital. The coastline of the fjord, along the inner banks of which Oslo was originally founded, is much indented, with cliffs falling sheer into the blue waters. The whole zone around Lyngør is now a protected area.

72-73

Lyngør, just a few miles to the south west of Oslo, is a part of the metropolitan area of the capital. It has recently been nominated as the best preserved village in Europe. Its architecture dates back to the days of the sailing ships, when it was a port of considerable importance.

FLYING HIGH NORWAY

74
Kongsberg lies in the county of Buskerud and is located south of Oslo along the River Numedalslågen. It is famous for its silver mines and for the Norwegian Mint, which is still located here today.

75
The picture shows Kirketorvet, the square with the Kongsberg church.

76-77

Larvik covers an area of some 204 sq. miles (530 sq. km) along the fjord that bears the same name; it flows into the Skagerrak in the county of Vestfold.

78

Larvik is a small city with a population of approximately 20,000; its most renowned citizen was the famous explorer Thor Heyerdahl – author of the book *Kon-Tiki* – who in 1947 crossed the Pacific Ocean from the coast of Peru to Polynesia on a primitive balsa-wood raft.

79

In this view of the end of the fjord one can see the little port of Larvik. A ferry service links the city with Denmark.

80 left and 81

With its covered area of some 24,778 sq. ft (2302 sq. m), its 75 rooms and 21 cellars, the Fritzøehus – near Larvik – is the largest private residence in all of Norway. It was built by the noted Norwegian architect Jacob Wilhelm Nordan between 1863 and 1865 in the style of a castle, which was very much the fashion of the time.

80 right

The gardens that form part of the Fritzøehus Park are an admirable cross between the international tradition and the Norwegian romantic style, which tends to conceal the intervention of man in favor of a more "natural" approach.

FLYING HIGH NORWAY

83

Kragerø has been a city since 1666. It has approximately 11,000 inhabitants and is the most southerly community in the county of Telemark, which is located in the south of the country, extending from the Hardangervidda plateau down to the coast.

84-85

The origins of Risør go back to 1500. These characteristic wooden houses date back to 1861, when they were rebuilt following the last great fire, which destroyed 284 homes.

86

Tønsberg, a city with slightly over 36,000 residents, is located in the county of Vestfold. This view shows the pedestrian bridge over the channel linking the islands of Nøtterøy and Tjøme; it can be opened when necessary.

87

The *Slottsfjelltårnet* at Tønsberg is the castle tower built in 1888 to replace the previous wooden one that had burned down in 1876. It stands 56 ft (17 m) high.

88-89
Arendal lies in the central part of
the Aust Agder in southern Norway.

90-91
Arendal has a population of approximately 39,000 and has always been known for its shipbuilding business.

92 left and right
Even from this view of the marina and the historic quarters of Arendal, where the fish market is held, one can appreciate how much of its history the city owes to the sea. Founded in the 16th century, by the end of the 19th century it had already become one of Norway's main naval centers. Arendal is today a notable tourist attraction.

93
The bell tower of Trinity Church stands out in this panoramic view of the historic center of Arendal.

94-95

Trinity Church, with a spire that rises 272 ft (83 m) high, dates from the 1800s. Some 1.4 million red bricks were needed to build the church, considered to be the symbol of Arendal.

96-97

Grimstad, a small town of some 19,000 inhabitants in the south of Norway, looks out onto the Skagerrak and is famous for having had the young Ibsen, as well as Knut Hamsun, winner of a Nobel Prize in Literature, as guests.

98 and 99
Kristiansand is famous for its shipyards; the traditional skills of shipbuilding date back to the city's origins.

100

Kristiansand, with its 70,000 inhabitants, accommodates many industries and is an important command center for the Norwegian Armed Forces.

101

To the left of the photograph can be seen the square outline, known as the *Quadratur*, of the original nucleus of Kristiansand, founded in 1641 by Christian IV, the king of Denmark-Norway.

FLYING HIGH NORWAY

103

The cathedral of Kristiansand was completely burnt down in 1880 in one of the frequent fires that hit the city from 1743 onwards. The cathedral we see here was built to resemble its predecessor.

104-105

Because of its sheltered position within the *skjærgård*, the archipelago of glacial skerries, on which stands a part of Kristiansand, the locality has always been a safe anchorage for ships navigating to and from Denmark.

106 and 107
Small wooden homesteads paint-
ed in various bright colors populate the areas surrounding Kristiansand. The southern region of
Norway, known as Sørlandet, is
typified by small islands and
rocky outcrops that give rise to an
intricate archipelago. In this part
of the Vest Agder are to be found
a number of small inhabited settlements, often interlinked by little
bridges, where boats are the only
certain means of transport.

FLYING HIGH NORWAY

109 and 110-111
The respect accorded to tradition is apparent every corner of Norway and even in the wooden houses in this small town on the Skagerrak, along the southern coast of the country near Kristiansand.

112
Egersund is a small city of approximately 10,000 inhabitants and the chief town of the Eigersund Kommune in the Rogaland region to the south west of the country. In Norway, a "Kommune" is an administrative entity similar to a province within a region.

114-115
Like Alesund, Egersund bases its economy on industries tied to the sea; with its excellent natural harbor, the town was considered to be Norway's largest producer of fish-related products down until 2005.

116-117
Stavanger, one of the most ancient and important cities of southwestern Norway, still has the typical concentric layout found in Scandinavian inhabited settlements dating from medieval times. Many small wooden houses still survive.

118
With the discovery of oil in the Norwegian Sea, Stavanger has been transformed from a city of fishermen into the capital of the black gold industry. Alongside its historic center, industrial areas have been developed.

119
The marina, with all its leisure crafts, and the long bridge are the twin symbols of modern Stavanger, a city of 170,000 inhabitants enjoying both a demographic and an economic expansion.

120
Stavanger became a bishopric in AD 1120. St. Svithun's Cathedral, destroyed by a fire in 1272, was rebuilt in a style combining both Romanesque and Gothic elements.

121
Following the reform of 1536, Stavanger was no longer a bishopric and therefore lost the greater part of its authority. Several religious buildings spread through the green areas of the city provide eloquent testimony of the historic vocation of this chief town of the Rogaland region.

122-123
Just as with many Norwegian cities, the main residential area of Stavanger is fairly extensive and takes in many islands as well.

124-125
Haugesund, with its 31,000 inhabitants, is famous throughout Norway for the numerous festivals held there, the most unusual of which is the Herring Festival.

126-127
The Karmsundbrua is the bridge that connects the insular part of the Rogaland region with its continental section; it is near Haugesund.

128 and 129
Haugesund is an important maritime transport center. According to legend, the city was built on foundations made of fish bones.

130-131
Bergen, with some 240,000 residents, is Norway's second largest city. Though badly damaged by fire in the early 1900s, it retains a prosperous and dignified look and remains a very pleasant city.

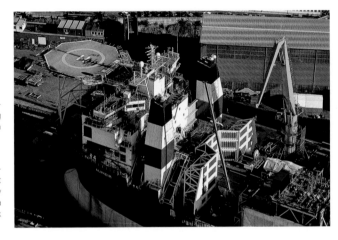

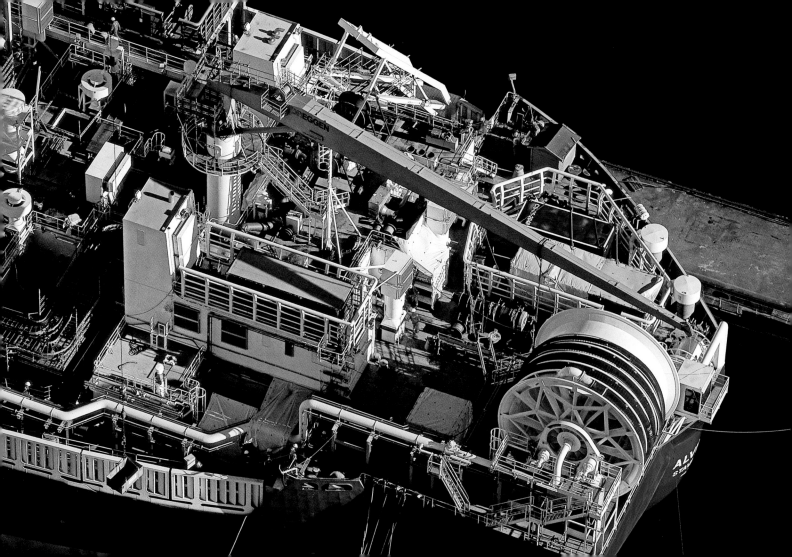

132 and 133

Bergen, with approximately 240,000 residents, is the second largest inhabited center of Norway. Even though badly damaged by fire at the start of the 1900's, it continues to be a very pleasant city with a prosperous and dignified look about it. Once a member city of the Hanseatic League, then an important religious center, it can boast several buildings of worship within its historic city center as well as hidden amongst the greenery of the city's parks.

134

Mariakirken is the most ancient church (and also monument) in Bergen, dating from the 12th century.

135

Bergenshus festning is the name of the medieval fortress built by King Håkan Håkansson at Bergen. It contains a very large hall for festivities that is considered to be amongst the most beautiful examples of the Gothic style in all of Norway.

136

In this view of Bergen can be seen the Puddefjorden (the arm of the sea to the left) and the Vågen, separated from each other by the point of Nordnes. In the foreground is the city park and, immediately to the left, the Grieghallen, the very beautiful concert hall in the shape of a piano.

137

The Fløybanan funicular railway climbs to the top of the Fløyfiell hill, 1050 ft (320 m) high. From here one overlooks Bergen and gains a panoramic view over the Byfijord and the Gulf of Vågen.

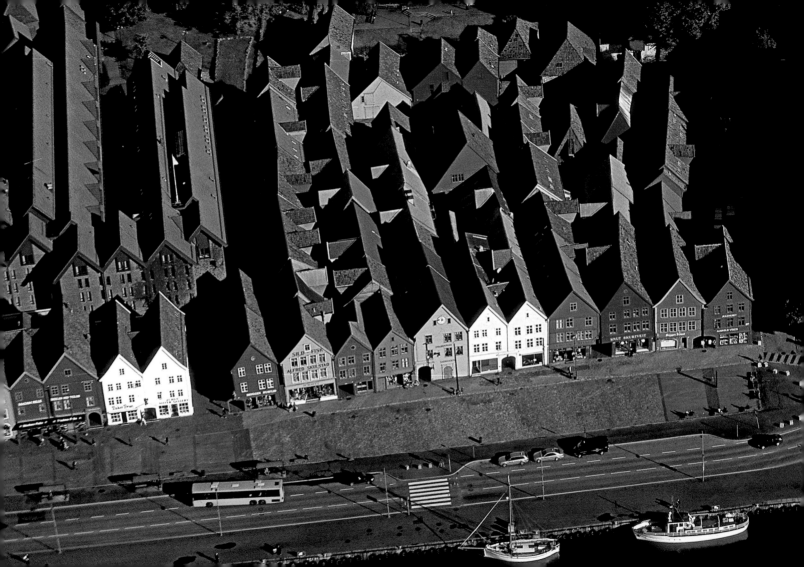

138-139
Between the 15th and 16th centuries, the Hanseatic League had its own port area in Bergen – the Bryggen – which it governed autonomously. UNESCO recently designated the Bryggen as a World Cultural Heritage site.

140-141
Always an important port, and today a rich and modern city,
Bergen is located on the southwestern coast of the country in
the county of Hordaland, of
which it is the administrative
capital. It is considered to be the
gateway to the fjords of Norway.

142

Mount Floyen overlooks the southern part of Bergen. Below can be seen the area given over to the new port.

143

In the center of Bergen many buildings bring to mind the Hanseatic golden age, both in Bryggen (to the left) and in Nordnes (to the right).

144-145

The well-ordered and spacious layout of Trondheim is directly due to the project prepared by General Caspar de Cicignon, who rebuilt the city at the end of the 17th century after a disastrous fire.

146
Located in the county of Sør-Trøndelag, Trondheim was built on the es-
tuary of the Nidv River and, with approximately 160,000 inhabitants, is
Norway's third city.

147
Along the banks of the Nidv rise the ancient warehouses of Trondheim
(above left). The port area is famous for its nightclubs.

148
The university buildings at Trondheim are modern and functional. This most southern of the great Norwegian cities adds some 30,000 university students to its own population.

The statue of King Olav (right) rises over the Market Square (left). The Viking king Olav Tryggvason founded the city in 997, building his palace there and proclaiming the city capital of Norway, with the name of Nidaros.

The Market Square stands at the center of Trondheim, a city with a breezy and modern air. Trondheim has suffered a number of fires over the centuries, the most destructive occurring in 1681. It was deliberately rebuilt with wide avenues to limit the damage from any future fires.

152-153
From the fortress of Kristiansen, which dominates Trondheim from a high point, one gains an impressive view of the city. The fortress was built by the Norwegian commander Johan Caspar von Cicignon, who became famous for having fought and won the battle of Vågen during the Second Anglo-Dutch War and also for having created the main fortified defences of Norway when the country belonged to Denmark.

154

Mollenberg is the old working class area of Trondheim, located on the east bank of the Nidv as it circles the historic center. Many of the old wooden houses built in the 18th and 19th centuries for the workers have been preserved.

155

Nidaros Cathedral, in Trondheim, was built at the turn of the 12th century. Inside the cathedral is the burial place of Olav, who brought Christianity to Norway and who was made a saint. On the strength of his cult, Trondheim became an important political and religious center.

156 and 157
In the Viking era, Munkholmen at Trondheim was the spot for executing capital punishment. A monastery was subsequently built there. Munkholmen is today a very popular place with the inhabitants of Trondheim, who come here to stroll along the strip of land that emerges from the island at low tide and to relax on the little beaches.

158
Narvik was totally destroyed during the Second World War and then rebuilt.

159
Narvik is the world's largest iron-ore shipping port. The great Swedish mines at Kiruna are linked to it by a railroad over which long trains carry endless supplies of the mineral.

160-161
Narvik's location, deep inside the Herjangsfjorden, makes it a well-protected natural port; the surrounding water never freezes.

162 left

The bridge in the foreground, the Tromsø Bru, is more than a half mile (1 km) long and links the two parts of Tromsø: the historic center and the old port, on the island of Trommsoya, with the residential areas of Tromsdalen, created on the mainland.

162 right

The old port was for a long time the heart of the city. Because of its location, Tromsø was the base for the whaling fleet which brought prosperity to this region.

163

Tromsø is located on the island of Tromsoya (from which it takes its name). It is a scientific center of great importance, with an academy specializing in arctic studies. Tromsø also has a famous planetarium.

164
Tromsø exists in a rather special location right at the extreme north of Norway, well above the Arctic Circle.

165
Tromsø has the world's "most northerly" university, distillery, botanical garden, Catholic diocese, and Protestant cathedral.

166

Placed at a fairly high latitude, Tromsø is famous for its midnight sun and for its snowfalls, that can easily reach a depth of 6-7 ft (2 m). Notwithstanding all this, the city is always perfectly organized and the roads scrupulously clean and passable.

167

A winter that lasts five months, temperatures below zero and snow for never less than 180 days of the year never seem to discourage the inhabitants of Tromsø, who have built up an excellent relationship with nature and who live willingly in the most secluded of localities.

THE INFINITE PATCHWORK

FLYING HIGH

FLYING HIGH NORWAY

169
Sjøvegan (left) is located on the coast of the Vågsfjord on the island of Hinnøya. Lyngør (right) is a tourist resort very well-known both in Norway and abroad.

July 2, 1893 was a significant date for the people of the remote towns and villages in the north of Norway. From the port of Trondheim the coastal steamer *Vesterålen* set out for the north, to Hammerfest, the very last outpost before the North Cape.

Thus was the opening of the "Hurtigrute" which, in Norwegian, means "fast road," a shipping route linking the coastal ports while bringing the long isolation of the northernmost provinces to an end. This initiative was an enormous success, greeted with celebrations, and for more than a century now the ships of the Hurtigrute have been navigating up and down the coast carrying passengers, mail and merchandise. There are now 11 vessels that service this route 365 days a year, linking 34 ports of call. Twelve days are needed to cover the entire route, which over the years has been extended to the south as far as Bergen and to the north until Kirkenes, at the border with Russia. And there are now over 500,000 tourists that make this journey.

The route follows the coastline, with such a spectacular and ever-varying panorama that it soon became known as "the most beautiful journey in the world." It was no longer just merchandise with a few sparse passengers, but tourists coming from all over the world to fill the ships. These ships were originally very spartan, essentially modified cargo vessels; given the growing success of the line, though, Hurtigrute vessels became a true fleet with the most up-to-date ships, increasingly large and comfortable, genuine cruise lines and no longer cargo boats. Even so, those who, like me, have traveled on one of the old historic

170
The highly indented Norwegian coastline is more low-lying toward the southern part of the country.

The Infinite Patchwork

vessels will have felt their great fascination, precisely because they were smaller and more "intimate." The limited space helped stimulate social togetherness while sitting out on the bridge, wrapped in a blanket with a glass of brandy in hand, as the spectacular Norwegian coast with its myriad forms and shades of color unfolded in front of your eyes.

The view from above is notably different from that as seen from the sea. Perspectives change and the steep rock faces that plunge into the sea no longer seem so dramatic. Distances become reduced and the intricate maze formed by the fjords, bays and channels now appears clear and precise. From the ships, however, perceptions give a distorted picture of reality and only the navigational instruments can ensure a safe and accurate passage. By way of compensation, man is reduced to his true insignificant dimension in the face of this wonder of creation.

There are three occasions when the ship leaves the calm coastal navigational waters, sheltered by offshore islands, and takes briefly to the open sea. The first is when the ship heads for Lofoten, a series of islands with their irregular and jagged peaks which, when seen at an angle, seem never ending until they reach Vesterålen. One stops at small fishing villages, welcomed by the cries of the gulls and other sea birds, disturbed by the ship's engines. Life on these islands is dependent on the sea for its food and for all links with the outside world. In fact, the racks built for drying out the stockfish and the various landing places all pepper the shoreline, while the fishing boats moored to their great colorful buoys rock gently, moving to the waves of the Norwegian Sea.

The second occasion is when, having left Hammerfest, the northernmost city in the world, the ship enters the Barents Sea and aims directly for the island of Magerøya, the site of the North Cape. Everyone knows of the North Cape, it was one of those epic journeys to be achieved by whatever means available, often desperate. The journey was invariably a great adventure because of the distance involved and also because the road was only asphalted in the mid-eighties.

The Infinite Patchwork

They came hitch-hiking, on motorbikes, on trucks perhaps converted into forerunners of the modern camper, even on bicycles and on foot. The important thing was reaching this headland which plummets steeply into the sea on the island of Magerøya, and which is often falsely described as the northernmost point of continental Europe. But this is not true, the title belonging in fact to the nearby peninsula of Knivskjellodden.

The North Cape has always been considered the northernmost point of the European road network because it is more readily accessible, as is demonstrated by the historic accounts left by the first explorers such as the *Northern Voyages* by Francesco Negri of Ravenna, dated as far back as 1633, or by Giuseppe Acerbi of Mantua, who published his *Diary* in 1799. Probably more important than these Italian "expeditions" was the publicity gained by the visit of the Swedish-Norwegian king, Oscar II, in 1873.

Whether it be Nordkapp or Knivskjellodden, the question never changes: why undergo so much discomfort to reach such a desolate and stony rock face, always exposed to strong winds, only to find a top-class tourist facility with prohibitive prices and from there turn the car around and go all the way back? The most obvious though scientific answer was given to me by a psychologist with whom I traveled in my years as a student of matters Scandinavian, when I paid for my books and practiced my language skills by accompanying groups on behalf of a tour operator. "The North Cape is a mental barrier," he told me. I have never really understood the meaning of these words but they were certainly highly relevant to the person that I had once met a few years earlier on a train from Stockholm to Narvik, when, quite by chance, I found myself for the first time heading for the North Cape. I had ended up on that train because I wanted to go to Finland but, on the way, had met up with a group of young Italians who urged me to join them as far as the North Cape, and so I accepted. Quite by chance, in the same compartment there was a retired man from Milan whose lifelong dream was to reach

The Infinite Patchwork

the headland and who had invested all his savings to make it come true. He was a likeable and peaceful type, spoke only the Milanese dialect and had a bulging wallet filled with cash. If he had not met up with us, he would have undoubtedly gone up to the nearest taxi driver, shown him all his money and simply said "North Cape." When he finally reached his destination I saw him cry like a baby, ask that a picture be taken of him and that was it, he turned to go back happy and contented.

A journey to the extreme north is a fantastic experience. Few things compare to the spectacle of the fjords cutting deep into the shoreline, with the intense blue colors of the Norwegian Sea dotted with the colorful floats of the salmon hatcheries and the white fishing boats. Or with the numerous, tiny rocky islands which shelter the coast, inhabited only by seabirds. The sky varies incessantly from the most intense blue to the most threatening grey while the weather changes constantly. Among my records, I have two photographs taken one after the other from the same position. In the first one it is sunny, in the other the rain is falling. These were taken within 30 seconds, barely time to advance to the next frame! It's a continuous process of putting on and taking off raincoats and sweaters because, in summer, temperatures can shoot from 36° to 86° Fahrenheit (2° to 30° Celsius) in very little time. Just one cloud covering the sun and the temperature plummets.

The third and last time that the ship takes to the open sea is upon leaving Honningsvåg and heading for the great fjord at the head of which lies Kirkenes, the destination for one journey and the beginning of another.

If you ask people what Norway is known for, they all reply, "The fjords." These are nothing other than the

The Infinite Patchwork

ancient valleys formed by the glaciers which have filled with water as the ice melted. For this reason the longest and steepest fjords are to be found in the south of Norway, extending up as far as Ålesund. The farther north one goes, the lower the country becomes, with the walls of the fjords less steep and the peaks less high. The zone where the fjords are located can be divided, from north to south, into four major regions: in the Møre and Romsdal area, within 6 miles (10 km) one passes from the Atlantic coast to the inner reaches of the deepest fjords, from a relatively mild climate supporting agriculture to a more severe continental type. In this area, mountain peaks rise almost vertically from sea level and some of the most breathtaking views in Norway can be found here, such as the Trollstigen road with its sharp curves or the broad rocky face of the Trollveggen.

In the Sogn and Fjordane region the Sognefjord can be seen, the longest in the world, which stretches for about 125 miles (200 km) from the coast up to the Jotunheimen mountain range, and the Jostedalsbreen glacier.

The Hordaland is the area around Bergen where the Hardangervidda, the most extensive upland plain in Norway, drops suddenly down to the fjord. To the north the countryside is steep, wild and almost totally uninhabited while in the more southern part of the region lies Hardanger Fjord, with its numerous waterfalls cascading directly into the sea and its many islands.

The Rogaland fills the southernmost part of the Norwegian fjord area and has a highly indented coastline. It is in this area that the long and narrow Lysefjord can be found, with its famous Prekestolen, or "Pulpit," a rock face which plunges perpendicularly for nearly 2000 feet (600 meters) directly into the sea, as well as the only plain in Norway, near Jæren, typified by its long beaches and sandy dunes.

176-177
The southern coastline near Oslo is marked by very deep inlets and by a large number of rocky outcrops and small islands, which are only uncovered at low tide.

178
The small islands which can be found in the Oslofjord are occupied
by the little summer homes of the residents of the capital.

179
Right where the Oslofjorden narrows – a key strategic position – the
island of Oscarborg is home to a fortress of great importance during the
Second World War; the torpedo boats, which sank the German battleship
Blucher in 1940, set off from this point.

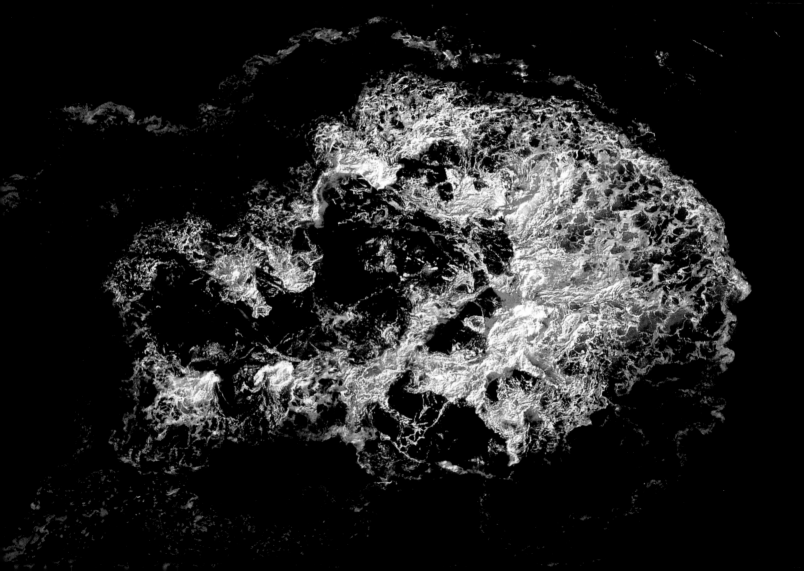

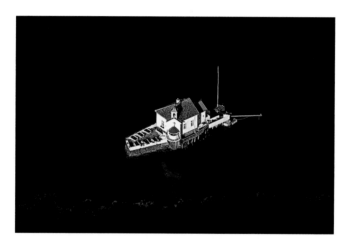

180
The sea breaks over one of the many rocky outcrops off the southern coast of Norway, near Oslo.

181
It takes only a handkerchief of rock to build a church and cemetery. Here we are in the heart of the Oslofjord, on the outskirts of the city.

182-183
The elongated island of Jomfru-
land has one of the most beautiful and famous beaches in Norway, particularly loved by bird-
watching enthusiasts. The play of
the currents in this extremely
fragmented coastal zone to the
west of the Oslofjorden has fa-
vored the formation of a sandy
littoral.

184 and 185
The relatively mild climate of southern Norway allows the woods to come right down to the water's edge. Here we are near Tønsberg.

186-187
The coastline of Mølen, near the village of Helgeroa, carries all the marks of the workings of the ancient glaciers; this region is in fact famous for its round stones of glacial origin, which have become much sought-after souvenirs.

188-189
A jumble of reefs and low islands is typical of the Norwegian coast near Arendal.

190 and 191
The coasts around Helgeroa and Nevlunghavn, villages that come under the administrative jurisdiction of Narvik, alternate high cliffs (to the
left) with low sandy islands of glacial origin (see photo to the right, in
the background).

192-193
Minuscule cottages have proliferated along this stretch of the coast of
Aust Agder between Lyngør and Risør, where the rock marches di-
rectly into the sea.

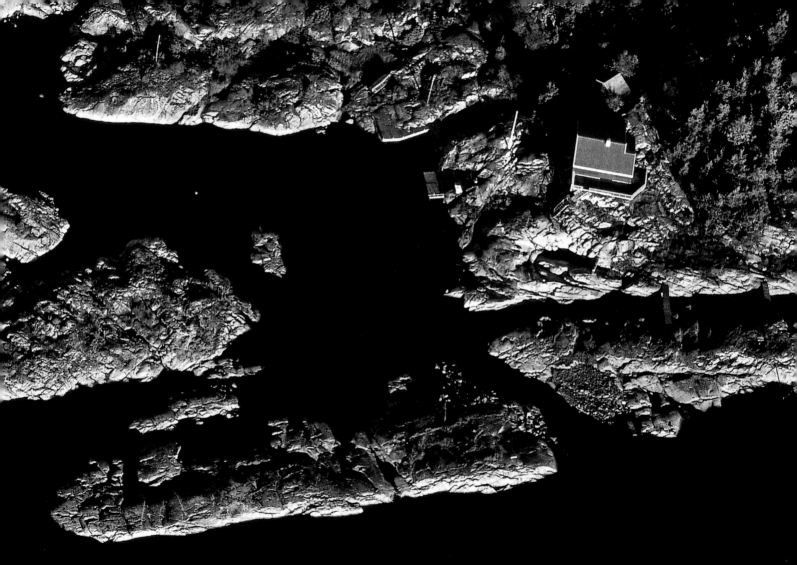

194 and 195
Norwegians love secluded places, in close touch with nature. They are therefore not afraid to build their small homes directly on rock or on a tiny island little larger than an outcrop, as can be seen from these photographs taken in the Aust Agder county in southern Norway.

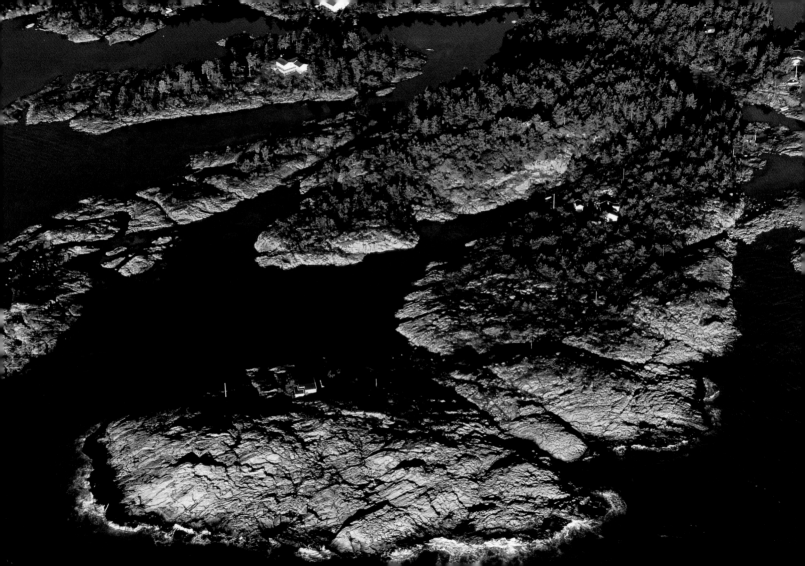

196
The coastline of Aust Agder is low-lying and rocky, and suffers the incessant action of the wind.

197
The Tromøybrua Bridge is approximately 1300 ft long (400 m) with a 780 ft span (240 m).

198-199
The Telemark Canal runs through the center of the wooded region, that carries the same name, and links the inland lakes to the sea.

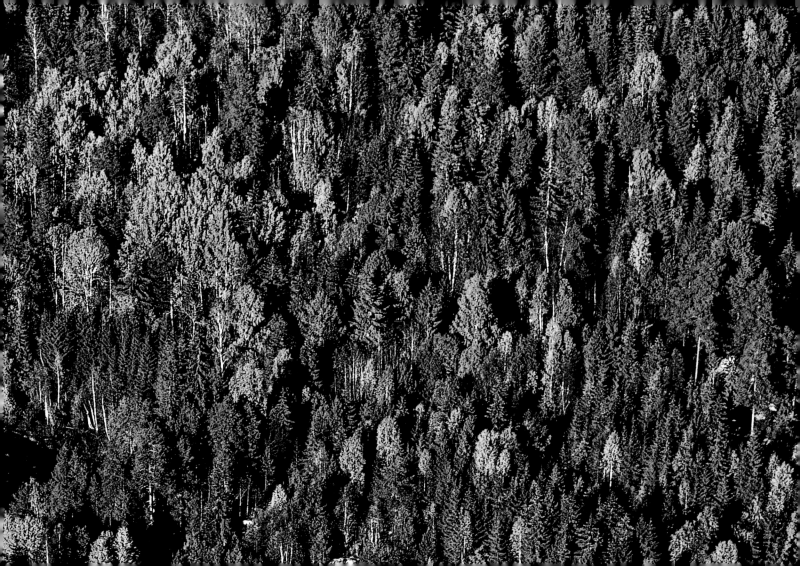

200-201
The coast near Arendal benefits from the effects of the Gulf Stream, as it is clearly proven by the thick vegetation.

202-203 and 204-205
Near Egersund the shoreline clearly bears evident traces of the actions of both wind and sea; the worn-down rocks and the salt water offer few concessions to any woodlands, which are only to be found farther inland.

206-207
The southern coast of Norway is characterized by its emerging cliffs. The presence of lighthouses such as that shown here continues to be a necessity for navigation, even in these times of satellite guidance.

208 and 209
The stretch of sea near the Egersund coast is particularly dangerous for navigation because of the many submerged rocks. Many ships have been wrecked in these treacherous waters.

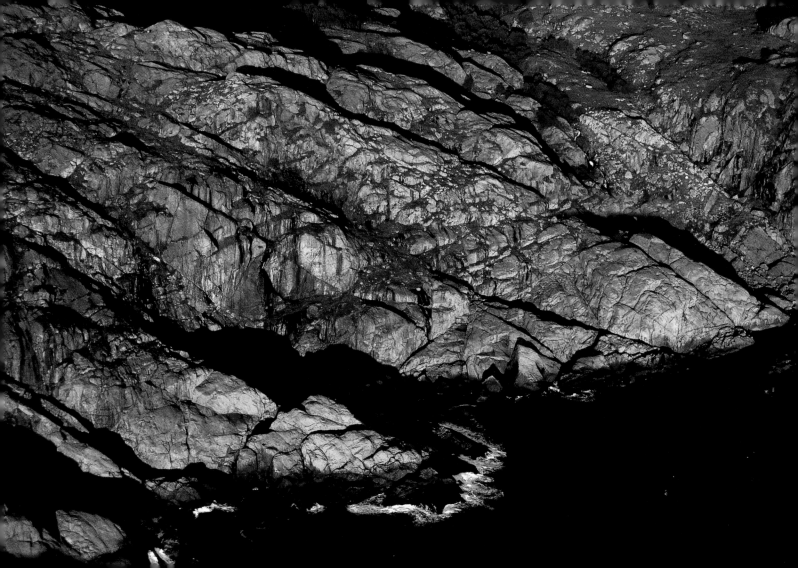

210
Facing the coast between Stavanger and Haugesund, in the Vestlandet, are a number of islands – the so called Skjærgården – which form a barrier between the dry land and the open sea.

211
The relative mildness of the climate in southwestern Norway favours a flourishing agricolture.

212-213
Even this particularly rocky stretch of coastline in Rogaland, between Stavanger and Haugesund, accommodates its share of small cottages by the sea.

214-215
The cultivated fields between Stavanger and Ahugesund bear witness to the positive influence of the Gulf Stream on the climate.

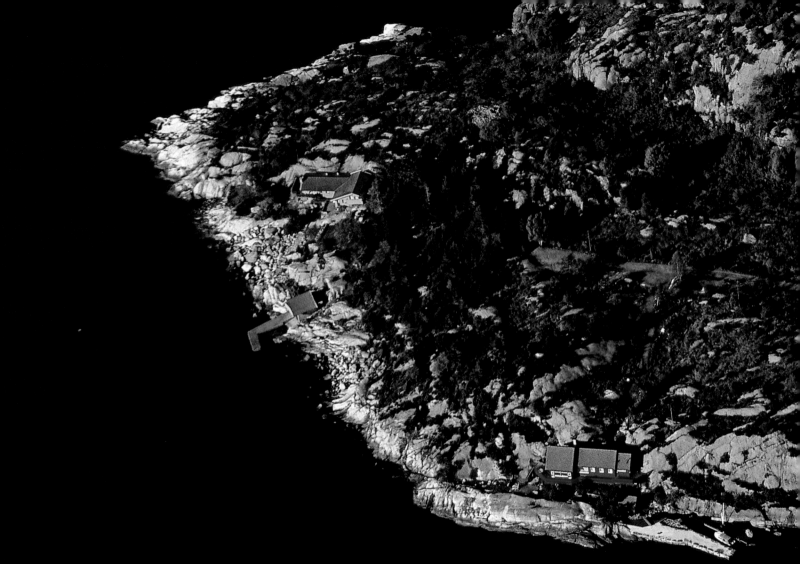

FLYING HIGH NORWAY

217

The archipelago of which Kalvoina is the main island, is situated in the Broknafjorden facing Stavanger, on the route taken by the ferries linking the Stavanger peninsula with Rogaland. These islands too enjoy a climate moderated by the passing of the Gulf Stream, as is clearly evident by the thick growth of this forest.

218

Norway enjoys a singular stroke of good fortune: an incredibly large expanse of coastline in relation to the size of the country. The presence of numerous, many-branched fjords and the spread of inhabited settlements along the coasts have, over the centuries, developed in the Norwegians a genuine passion for the sea. So it is by no means unusual – as can be seen in this photograph – to discover small villas immersed in the greenery a few yards from the sea, each with its own little pier and every other comfort for recreational navigation.

220 and 221 right

The Lysefjorden is one of Norway's most famous fjords, noted for its rocky cliff faces that
in some places fall sheer into the water from
over 3300 ft (1000 m).

221 left

This spectacular fjord, wedged between the
mountains of the mainland, is known as the
Nålen or "Needle" because of its long, pointed
and narrow shape.

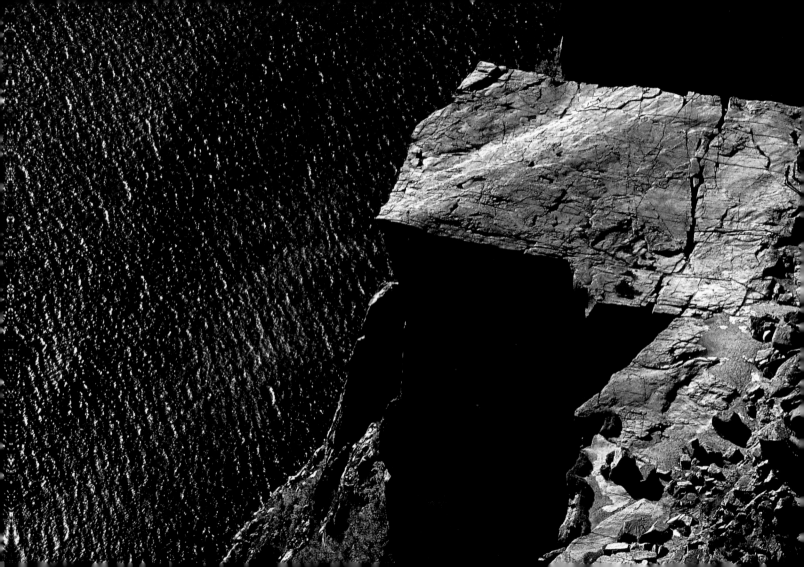

222-223

The Preikestolen, or "Pulpit," offering one of the most famous panoramic views in the world, is a granite terrace located 2000 ft (600m) sheer above the Lysefjorden. The vertical crevice in the foreground was caused by atmospheric factors and is a consequence of the geological phenomena that are continually modifying the appearance of the Norwegian fjords.

224 and 225
The Lysefjorden is one of the wildest fjords in the world. The dark color of the waters is an indication of their depth, which can reach 1500 ft (450 m). The rocks are of granite, and this explains the gorge-like shape and the range of color that makes it a popular tourist attraction.

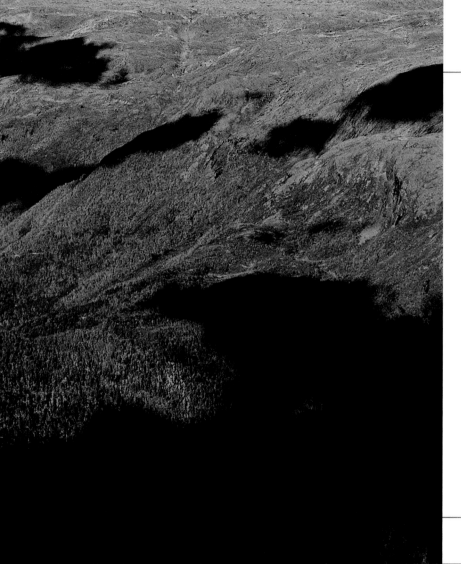

226-227

It is said that the name Lysefior-
den means "Luminous Fjord,"
where "luminous" stands for the
coloring; it represents an ac-
knowledgment of the spectacular hues of the granite which
forms the shores of this mar-
velous part of Norway, just a few
miles from Stavanger.

228 and 229
Glacier meets the sea; the Hardangerfjord laps up against the Folgefonna glacier, one of the most famous in Norway.

230-231
A 7 mile (11 km) tunnel excavated under the Folgefonna glacier links
Eitrheim with Mauranger. It previously took more than four hours to travel
between the two locations.

232

The Hardangerfjorden, 110 miles (179 km) long and 2600 ft (800 m) deep, is the fourth largest fjord in the world and the second in Norway after the Sognefjord. The glaciers overlooking the fjord are all that remains of the immense ice caps which, during their gradual migrations, contributed to the formation of the fjord.

233

The Folgefonna glacier is, in terms of its dimensions, Norway's third largest. It has a surface area of some 82 sq. miles (214 sq. km).

234-235

The highest point of the Folgefonna is 5450 ft (1662 m) above
sea level and its lowest 1310 ft
(400 m). In between lies a veritable sea of white, blasted by incessant winds.

236 and 237
The entire territory occupied by the Folgefonna was declared a National Park in 2005. The park also takes in part of the fjord and three glaciers: the Nordre (10 sq. miles / 26 sq. km), the Midtre (3.5 sq. miles / 9 sq. km) and the Sønde Folgefonna (65 sq. miles / 168 sq. km). This part of Norway has enjoyed its fair share of tourism starting from the 1800's; among its more famous visitors can be counted the tour-packaging pioneer Thomas Cook.

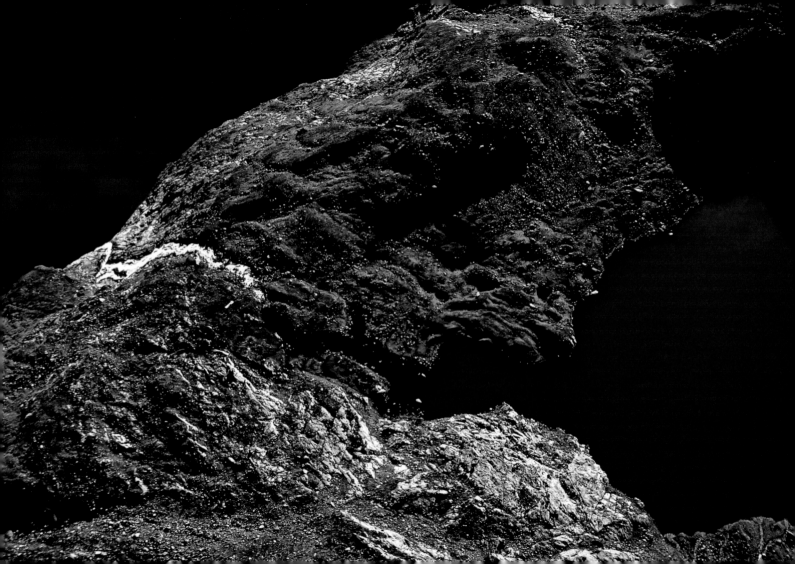

238 and 239
The waters from the melting of the Folgefonna glacier cascade down into the
fjord over high, spectacular waterfalls. In
the 1800s, the savage fascination of
these landscapes moved and inspired
many important Romantic artists.

240
The formation of the three glaciers making up the Folgefonna dates back some 2500 years, in response to the combined action of abundant snowfalls and particularly severe temperatures.

241
The effect of the wind creates an unusual ripple effect on the surface of the Folgefonna. The relatively mild seasons have led to a shrinking of part of the glacier, while at the same time promoting the growth of a summer ski season.

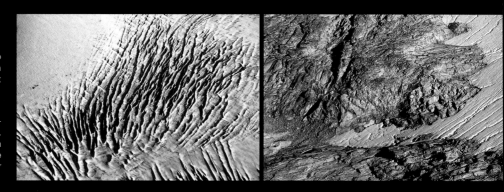

242-243

At the foot of the Hardangerfjorden, the mild temperatures allow fruit trees to grow. The climate and the fertility of the soil, inherited from the glaciers, have transformed this part of Norway into a sort of garden, even from as far back as the Viking era.

244 and 245
The Husnesfjorden forms part of the immense water system that is dominated by the Hardangerfjorden. It is included in the southern part of the peninsula where the Folgefonna glacier is to be found.

246

The Husnesfjorden opens out onto the Hardangerfjorden just beyond the small city of Sunde. In this extensive and many-branched network of inlets one can enjoy an incomparable landscape.

247

The Hordaland is the district of which Bergen is the chief town. It is considered the fjord region par excellence. Here the indelible traces left by the march of the glaciers is apparent in the gorges and the fissures, infiltrated by the waters of the ocean.

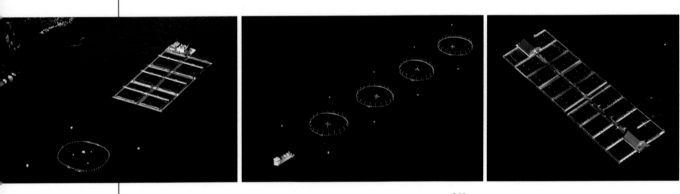

248
These fish farms were photographed near Rubbestadneset, in the Hordaland. The annual production of shellfish and farmed fish now amounts to some 600,000 tons and is certain to increase seeing that Norwegian farmed fish have become very popular in recent years, even in such a demanding market as that for sushi in Japan.

249
Fish is the Norwegian national dish. To protect the natural resources of the sea ever more space is being given over to fish farming, which ensures a neutral effect on the environment. The photograph was taken in the Hordaland, between Haugesund and Bergen.

250

In western Norway it frequently happens that only a thin wall of rock separates the salt water of the sea from the fresh waters of a lake, as can be seen in this fjord just a few miles from Bergen.

251

The incredibile ramifications found in the fjord area around Bergen are an inheritance from past geological eras: the invasion of the sea into the valleys carved by the glaciers has been responsible for the unpredictable shapes found today.

252

This view shows the labyrinth of small islands that characterize the bay of Bergen. The varying colors of the water are clearly evident and are due to the greater or lesser depth of the sea and to its degree of saltiness.

253

Bergen is a city with a rich history. Thanks to trade and fishing a number of families became extremely wealthy, and were able to build the sort of luxury homes that are shown in the photograph.

254-255

A crescent-shaped island offers an ideal landing spot for a sailing boat during the short Norwegian summer. Low, sandy shores are commonly found along this stretch of the Hordaland coast, between Rubberstadneset and Bergen.

256
The sand combines with the water creating playful effects of color along the coast near Rubberstadneset: the cultivated fields show that the climate is relatively mild.

257
Rubbestadneset is noted for its fish breeding along the inner coast of the island of Bømlo, in the Hordaland between Haugesund and Bergen.

258-259
Even slightly farther south from Bergen, toward Haugesund, the coastline is very much indented but rich in vegetation.

260 and 261
A villa for the nobility, its tower with a panoramic view and its landing-
place emerge from the thick vegetation on this small peninsula near
Bergen: a further sign of the prosperity evident in this territory
presided over by Norway's second city.

FLYING HIGH NORWAY

263
Many of the small islands that one comes across while traveling around Hordaland near Bergen are totally or almost totally uninhabited. During the brief summer at these latitudes, they become a major attraction for sailing enthusiasts.

FLYING HIGH NORWAY

265
A dirt road, built on a narrow strip of land, connects this tiny island to the mainland. It is not unusual to come across scenes like this along the fjord of Trondheim, in the northwest of Norway: here the cold ocean waters penetrate deeply into the Norwegian coastline, offering landscapes of singular beauty.

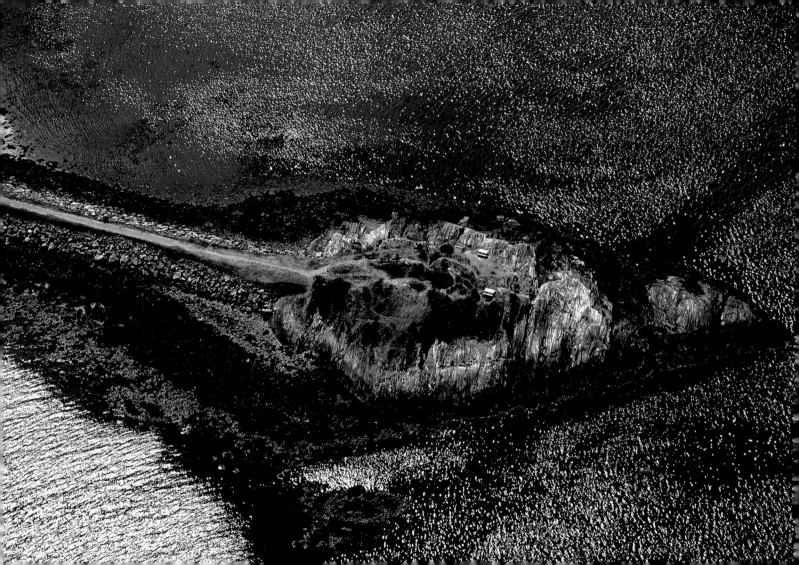

266 and 267
The Ofotfjorden, in Nordland, is 48 miles (78 km) long and descends to 1814 ft (553 m) at its deepest point. The fjord is surrounded by mountains of up to 5600 ft (1700 m). At its eastern end stands Narvik.

268 and 269
The island of Trømsoya is located in the far north of Norway. The climate is extremely severe even though partly mitigated by the effects of the Gulf Stream. Trømsoya in spring still looks like this: covered by a white blanket that doesn't seem to want to go away.

270

White and blue are the springtime colors in the county of Troms: the snow persists until the end of May while in the waters circling the island the freezing currents of fresh water from the melting snows leave their turquoise brush-strokes.

271

From the entrance to the Ofotfjord one can catch a glimpse of the mountains that define its bottom end. The Ofotfjord is the longest fjord in Nordland and the fourth in the country.

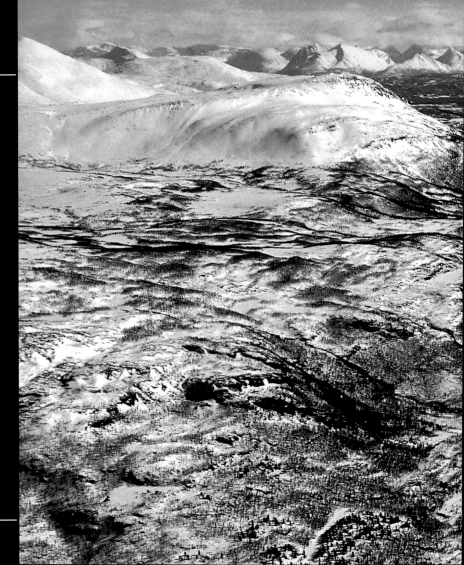

272-273
The coastline of the county of Troms, much indented as in the rest of western Norway, faces onto the Norwegian Sea. The territory of the county is predominantly mountainous.

274 and 275
Because of the severity of the climate, even Troms county's few flat areas remain uncultivated. Livestock raising and fishing fuel the coastal
and island economy, which is not helped by the poor state of most of
the roads: for the greater part of the year the inhabitants use aircrafts
or boats for travelling around.

276 and 277

The Ofotfjord during the thaw offers the spectacle of nature, in all its savagery, coming to life. But in fact life never stops in this part of Norway: enriched by all its branching waterways, the Ofotfjord is an unspoiled area very much appreciated by shoals of herring, mackerel and cod and also by killer whales, otters, sea eagles and a wide variety of shellfish.

278

The Vågsfjorden benefits from temperatures that are particularly mild even for these latitudes, allowing agriculture to flourish. The extremely fertile soil also helps.

279

The Vågsfjorden is located on the island of Hinnøya which, with its 850 sq. miles (2200 sq. km), is the largest in Norway and forms part of the Vesterålen group of islands.

280

At the mouth of the Ofotfjord, the salt waters of the Norwegian Sea meet the fresh waters coming from inland areas; the resulting currents are extremely rich in nutriment and are very much appreciated by the fish.

281

Harstad is the capital of the island of Hinnøya. This small town of little more than 20,000 inhabitants on the shores of the Vågsfjord, is an important center not only for the military but also for the oil industry.

282 and 283
Sjøvegan was founded at the point where the salt waters of the Salangen meet with the fresh waters of the Nervatnet, this latter collecting the water from the melting snowfields of the neighboring mountains. A canal which crosses the city links up these two basins.

284-285
Magerøya is Norway's most northerly island and home to North Cape (Nordkapp). In the foreground can be seen the town center of Honningsvåg, which contends with Hammerfest, still in Norway, the role of being the most northerly city in the world.

286-287
Whether or not it is the northernmost point in all of Europe, Nordkapp can take consolation from
the more than 100,000 visitors
that it receives annually from all
over the world, arriving by the
most disparate and desperate
means.

288 and 289
Magerøya in Norwegian means "skinny island" because absolutely nothing grows here. Just lichens for the summer grazing of the reindeer.

290-291
Magerøya is free of snow only from June to August. Then a white blanket covers it for the remaining nine months.

292 and 293

New and old tracks intersect on the island of Magerøya, in the extreme north of Norway. Fresh and salt waters meet seasonally in the estuaries (see left and on next page); roads built for tourists cut through the mountains to carry the people toward North Cape (to the right).

294-295 and 296-297

Strips of land alternate with rocky cliffs along the coast of Magerøya, on the route toward North Cape.

298, 299 and 300-301
To the east of North Cape, along the promontory that separates the Norwegian Sea from the Barents Sea, the fury of atmospheric forces and the millenarian pressures of the ice have carved the coastline into its present shape: excavating, carving and leveling it.

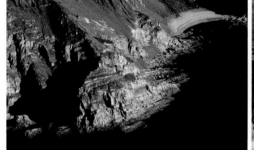 

FLYING HIGH NORWAY

303

Contrary to its reputation, North Cape is not in fact the most northerly point in Europe: at a latitude of 71° 11' 08", the "roof" of the continent is the promontory of Knivskjellodden, also located on the island of Magerøya. If we wish to be pedantic, the most northerly "continental" point in Europe is Cape Nordkinn, on the peninsula of Nordkynn.

FLYING HIGH NORWAY

305
The Tanafjord, which takes its name from the similar sounding River Teno which flows into this long and narrow bay, is considered the very best place for salmon fishing. In reality this fjord, which lies just to the south of the Nordkynn Penininsula, is of very great interest to geologists, who can study the original composition of the rocks, fully exposed by the timelessly incessant movement of the glaciers.

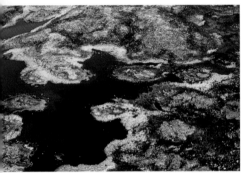 

306 left
The peninsula of Porsanger is uninhabited and there are only a few fishermen's settlements along the European Highway E69 that runs along the east coast and continues on to Nordkapp.

306 right
Only 4500 people live in the Porsangerfjorden, with 3000 of these in the main town, Lakselv. There is about one inhabitant per square kilometer.

307
The Porsangerfjord is from 6 to 12 miles (10 to 20 km) wide and extends in a north to south direction for 76 miles (123 km).

308
The freezing waters of the Tanafjord witnessed violent submarine battles between Germans and Russians during the Second World War.

310-311

The Tanafjorden is the most northerly in all Norway. Here we are well within the Arctic Circle, where the snow does not melt until late in June – and begins to fall again in September.

WHERE
MAN DARES

FLYING HIGH

313
The Vestfjorden (left) is in fact an arm of the sea separating the
mainland from the Lofoten Islands (to the right a view of Svolvær).

It is probably the only place in the world where one is obliged to go out armed. Not for self-defense against criminals, who are practically non-existent at this latitude, but against assaults from the polar bears which roam freely on the streets and around the homes of Longyearbyen; this is the "metropolis" of Svalbard, with its 1800 residents and 30 miles (50 km) of roads and which is also home to the *Sysselmann*, the governor placed there by the Norwegian state. Aside from the capital, there are two other populated centers: Ny Alesund, the northernmost village in the world with fewer than 100 residents, and Sveagruva, another 200 souls lost in the emptiness.

This archipelago is the last semi-inhabited territory (there are only 2500 people) before the North Pole. It consists of a group of islands measuring 12,957 sq. miles (62,050 sq. km) located in the Arctic Ocean, between the latitudes of 74° and 81° North. The climactic conditions are extreme, with cold and snow for the greater part of the year and the polar night lasting from the end of October to the beginning of January.

One may wonder what humans are doing in Svalbard, a land suited only for polar bears. In ancient times (and the islands were already known in Vikings times) these territories hosted hunting bases for whales and fur animals; but then a little over a century ago, in 1906, the American John M. Longyear founded a coal mining company here

314
A blanket of snow covers Austvågøya, camouflaging the
houses at Kabelvåg.

Where Man Dares

and gave his name to the area. Nowadays coal has lost its importance. There are still 700 Russian miners living and working in Barentsburg, a Russian enclave within the Norwegian territory. Only the proverbial Norwegian efficiency could have succeeded in transforming a pile of rocks and ice with no connecting roads between its populated centers into a livable space, equipped with a hospital, sporting facilities, libraries and community centers.

While outside conditions are certainly harsh, the interiors of buildings are constructed to ensure maximum comfort. They have insulated double-glazed windows and also anterooms for changing clothes. No one should be surprised at the sight of natives walking around shops and stores in their slippers. Taking off one's shoes before entering a building is a typical Svalbard tradition. It is a custom dating back to when the coal mines were still working and it was in fact adopted to avoid tracking black dust, mud and snow all over the place. To this day, one takes off one's shoes when entering a building and the local residents expect foreigners to comply with their practices.

In recent years tourism has discovered this last outpost of wilderness, though it is certainly not a destination for just anybody. There are very strict safety rules to be observed. If anyone decides to go out alone, besides carrying a gun to fend off bears, he always has to notify the police or the hotel management of his movements. The weather conditions change so radically and so rapidly that in a matter of seconds the sun can give way to a snowstorm – and getting lost in these conditions means certain death.

Despite seeming not the most hospitable of places, the Lofoten and Vesterålen islands – which are the area's natural continuation – have been known and inhabited for centuries, thanks to the abundance of fish in their waters. They are a string of islands scattered in the middle of the Norwegian sea at the level of the Arctic Circle, with sharp peaks that hurl themselves into the sea, with strong winds

Where Man Dares

blowing incessantly and weather conditions that can turn within ten minutes from sunny and calm to fiercely tempestuous, with 50-ft (16-m) waves and stormy seas. The climate is so changeable that it not surprising to see snow in June and summery temperatures in November. All depends on the winds and the currents.

There are six currents (they are, from east to west: *Raftsundet, Gimsøystraumen, Sundklakkstraumen, Nappstraumen, Sundstraumen* and *Moskenesstraumen*) all extremely powerful and dangerous, being caused by the violent impact of waters meeting over a seabed of various depths in the intricate pattern of islands, islets and rocky outcrops. The history of the Lofoten Islands is studded with all the victims of this perpetual battle between the sea and the fishermen.

Svolvær is the capital of Lofoten which, with its 4000 inhabitants, is a "metropolis" when compared to the small villages on the coast inhabited by a few dozen people. It is a very ancient town. Its origins date back to the Vikings but there have been findings dating back 3-4000 years. The original nucleus of modern Svolvær is the small island of Svinøya where, in 1828, the very first commercial ventures were opened: a bakery and the telegraph office. The store, called Krambua, still exists to this day. Like all other villages inhabited by Norwegian fishermen, this area around the harbor is also full of *rorbuer*, the typical wooden houses that serve simultaneously as homes and shelters for boats and fishing equipment. Since fishing has now become a much bigger undertaking, the *rorbuer* are mostly used as vacation homes to rent to tourists.

Everything on these islands revolves around fish, and one in particular: cod. Almost 90 percent of the stockfish eaten in Italy comes from here. What occurs in the small harbors of the archipelago amounts almost to an assembly line. During the fishing season, which lasts from January to April, the fresh fish within few hours becomes stockfish, ready for drying in the open and rain of these latitudes. It

FLYING HIGH NORWAY

318
The Lofotens (here is a small island near Svolvær) are a
paradise of nature and a great tourist resource for Norway.

is in fact the Lofoten Islands cod that led to the strong gastronomic tie with Italy. The dried cod from Lofoten has been known in Italy for almost six centuries, when a Venetian merchant lost his bearings in those waters and, rescued and fed, brought back 60 dried cod to his country. Svolvær is in fact twinned with Ancona and one of the types of dried cod takes its name from that particular city of the Marche region.

Once having reached the maximum limit for the sustainable catch, the industry has started to research the possibilities of fish farming. The Lofoten islands have proven to be an ideal choice for this activity. The numerous inlets, with their shallow waters, make it easy to spread the farming nets. After the initial experiments with salmon, fish farming is slowly extending to take in shellfish and other species, so that now the cold, deep blue waters are dotted with the colorful red, yellow and fuchsia buoys that mark out the fish farming areas.

Where there are fish there are also numerous other species of animals feeding off them, which explains why the Lofoten islands are now a nature sanctuary. The residents have taken the opportunity to exploit for tourist purposes the interest in sea animals, and the islands have become an important tourist destination for the close-up observation of whales, killer whales and sea birds of all kinds, such as the powerful sea eagle or the cormorant, which is considered the symbol of Lofoten. Nature-oriented tourism is becoming an ever more powerful element in the economy of the islands, which will also benefit from the opening of an underwater tunnel which will end their traditional isolation and provide a rapid connection to the mainland, whatever the condition of the sea.

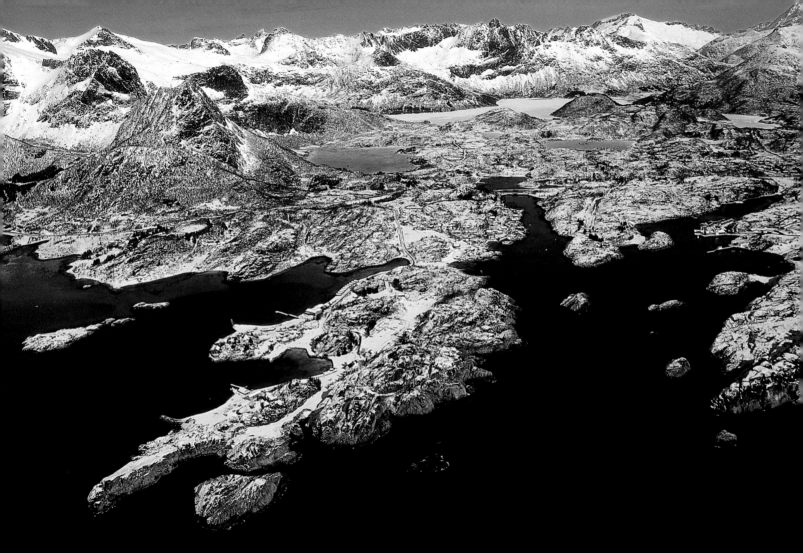

FLYING HIGH NORWAY

320 and 321
Summers on Austvågøya, in the Lofotens, last for two months during which the temperature can even reach 68-77°F (20-25°C). During the rest of the year snowfalls are frequent, even abundant, as can be seen from these pictures taken in the spring.

322-323
Kabelvåg has approximately 2000 inhabitants. In mediaeval times this was the most populated region in Scandinavia because of the fishing in the extremely well-stocked waters around the Lofotens.

324

The ancient town of Kabelvåg dates back to the beginning of the 12th century; it was given the name of Vågan when founded by Øystein, the Viking king who built here a church and a shelter for the fishermen.

325

Kabelvåg is to be found on the southern coast of Austvågøya, one of the Lofoten Islands. Together with Svolvær and Henningsvær, it comes under the administrative center of Vågan.

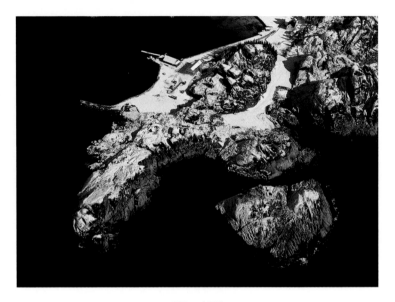

326 and 327
Austvågøya is the most easterly of the two large islands of Vågøy, in the
Lofotens (the other is obviously called Vestvågøya). The islands have
been inhabited since ancient times because of the abundance of fish
in these waters which, thanks to the influence of the Gulf Stream currents, maintain throughout the summer a temperature that barely reaches 68°F (20°C).

328 and 329
n the innermost bays (in this case near Kabelvåg) the water reezes over in winter. Nearer the open sea, the Gulf Stream keeps he waters clear of ice. In those egions less exposed to this current, winter temperatures as low as -28°F (-35°C) have been ecorded.

330 and 331

On this small archipelago stands the little community of Henningsvær, a village on the edge of Austvågøya enjoying great success with tourism. Its winter population of some 500 becomes almost 2000 in summer, when the Lofotens are visited by crowds of tourists, attracted to these lands at the very confines of the civilized world.

FLYING HIGH NORWAY

333

Henningsvær, in the Lofotens, is a community of fishermen that has settled over a group of islands and outcrops within the Vestfjord. At its shoulder, Mount Vågakaillen falls sheer into the sea. The various hamlets of Henningsvær are interconnected by small footbridges, though a much larger bridge links the village to the main island, Austvågøya.

334-335
Lødingen is a trading center for
the Lofotens. It is located on the
Vestfjord, facing the open sea,
and is surrounded by mountains.

336
Sand ground down by the tides, salt and sea-weed all combine to provide playful color effects on the waters lapping the reefs of Lødingen.

337
The unusual profile of the coastline near Lødingen results from the actions of the tides and of the winds which blow almost uninterruptedly here. The color of the sea reflects the contrast between the dark freshwaters coming from the melting ice and the seawater, which is normally warmer and more turquoise-tinted.

338 and 339
Svolvær is the administrative center of the municipality of Vågan, in the
Lofotens. This is a small town of some 4200 inhabitants, and is the most
popular departure point for tourists visiting the islands.

340-341
In this overall view of Svolvær, on the shores of the Vestfjord, one can appreciate the two mountains immediately behind the city: the Fløyfjellet (on the right) and the Kjellbergtinden (more to the left).

342
The ferries that leave for the other islands of the archipelago depart from Svolvær, which is also an important fishing port. The large buildings that can be seen along the pier are the factories where the fish are processed.

343
Just like Svolvær, Hennigsvaer is also spread over several islands, linked by bridges and short viaducts built above the tide levels.

344

Many of the small islands of the archipelago where Svolvær is located, which are now given over to tourist residences, were originally occupied by the homes of the fisherman.

345

Fish have an enormous importance for the economy of Svolvær. Practically all of the cod imported by Italy will have been caught in the Lofotens and processed at Svolvær.

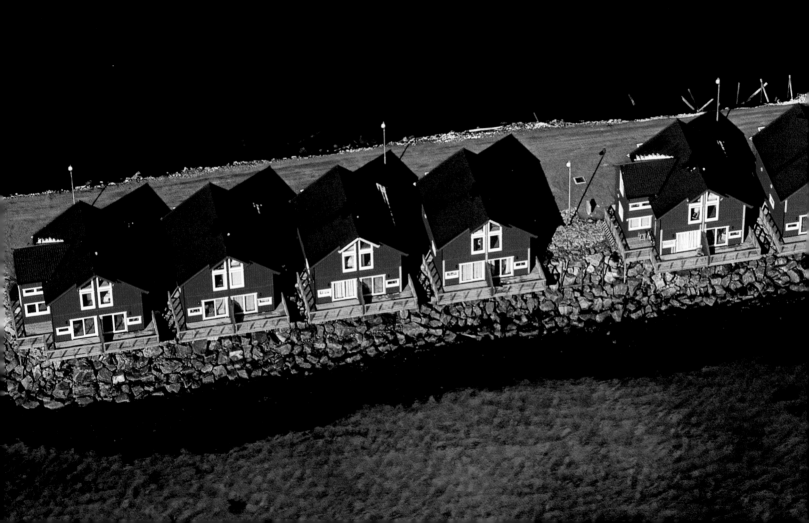

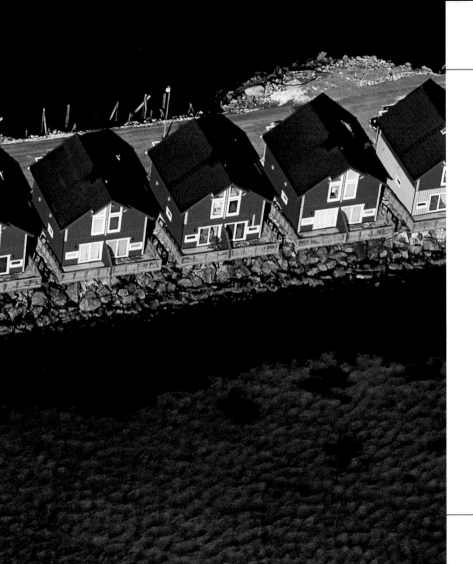

346-347
Rorbuer (the old homes of the fishermen, half a dwelling and half a shelter for boats and store-rooms) line the waterfront in Svolvær. Today they are rented out to tourists.

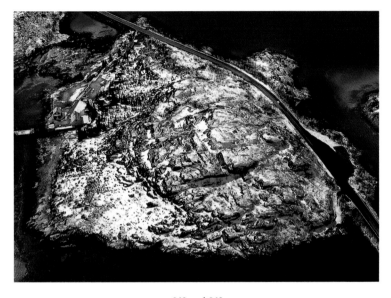

348 and 349
In Norway Svolvær is also known as "Lysebyen," the city of light. The
reason is identified with the very clear air, which tends to accentuate
all contrasts. This can clearly be seen in these pictures, taken on a
spring day just after a snowfall.

350 and 351
Almost 200,000 tourists come to Svolvær every year in the period between spring and autumn. Many of them do not use the town just as a gateway to the eastern Lofotens, but explore the immediately surrounding areas discovering the lakes, frozen over for nine months out of the year, and the spectacular mountains, still covered with snow in these photographs taken in spring.

352-353
In this photograph one can appreciate the wonderful position of Svolvær, protected by its encircling mountains from the freezing winds coming from the north.

354

Protected by the mountains to the north and the west, Svolvær and its immediate surroundings experience less fog and enjoy higher summer temperatures than the eastern parts of the Lofotens. These same mountains, however, are the cause of the intense rainfalls that typify the climate.

355

The highest mountain of the Lofotens is the Higravstinden, 3808 ft (1161 m). Slightly lower is the Svolværgeita – shown here in the foreground with Svolvær in the background – which was climbed for the first time in 1910.

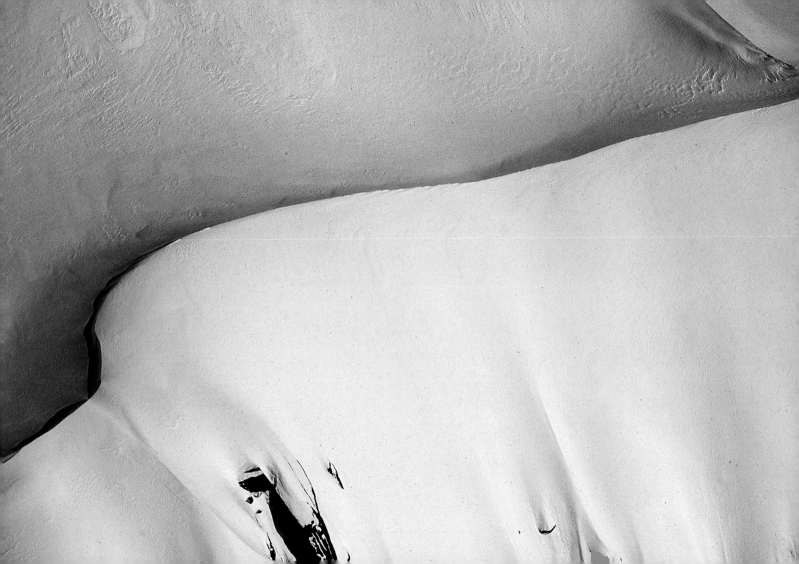

356 and 357 right
In winter the snow covers everything. In spite of the latitude, the winter temperatures of the Lofotens are not very severe, on average, although the snowfalls are fairly intense particularly on the islands farther to the east and on the Vestfjord.

357 left
The shadow of the helicopter is reflected on the snow in the vicinity of Svolvær. With this means of transport it has been possible to make these spectacular journeys in the skies over the Lofotens, which have been captured in these pictures.

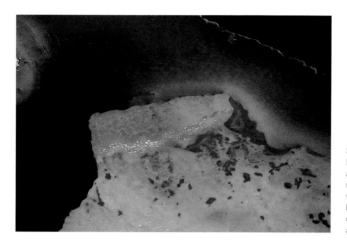

358 and 359
Spring is well advanced on the Lofotens; the thaw is becoming apparent. Where the ice is still melting, the water takes on a whitish tinge; where the sea is beginning to break through, the color turquoise starts to become apparent.

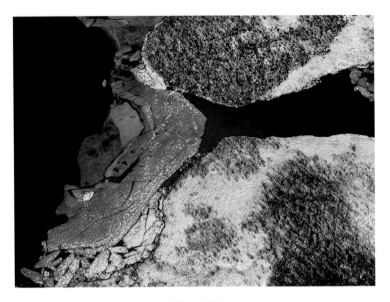

360 and 361
During the long winter, the ice has sealed off the arms of the Vestfjorden in a vise. Already in spring the effects of the Gulf Stream, which
flows along the coastline of northern Europe, can be felt in the Lofotens and the frozen sheets of ice begin to break up into thousands
of fragments, as can be seen in the photograph.

362 and 363

With the better weather, the various shades of green return to the Lofotens. The melting of the ice occurs first along the coasts of the Vestfjord, largely because of the mitigating effects of the sea currents. The fjords turn into giant channels, carrying the icy fresh waters down to the estuaries where they combine with the salt water in a kaleidoscope of colors. In the mountains, the effects of winter take longer to disappear: it will be May or June before the vegetation begins to show itself.

364 and 365
Still another view of Svolvær. The prosperity of this small town, deriving today mostly from tourism, was historically dependent upon its strategic position on the Vest-fjorden, an arm of the sea which every spring experiences migrations of huge shoals of cod from the Barents Sea.

366

Svolvær was born as a fishing village. Many traces of this adventurous past still remain, both in its typical wooden houses with their adjoining storerooms and also in the layout of the village itself, deliberately spread over small islands just off the seashore.

367

Svolvær competes with Stamsund and Bodø for the title of most important city of the Vestfjorden, that long channel that extends for 125 miles (200 km) as far as the island of Vesterålen.

368 and 369
Small beaches of white sand, rocks breaking out into a turquoise sea, reefs whipped by the wind, very few houses, primitive roads and tiny bridges linking minuscule islands; all this might appear in a photograph of a Caribbean 'cayo'; instead, we are talking of one of the many small and fragmented archipelagos facing the Vestfjorden.

370 and 371
Svalbard, whose main island is called Spitsbergen – meaning "pointed mountains" because of the particular shape of its profile – constitutes the last inhabited outpost before reaching the North Pole. The
greater part of the internal areas of the main island is permanently
covered by glaciers.

372 and 373
Svalbard, an archipelago in the Arctic Sea, constitutes the most northerly part of Norway. At this latitude the islands are exposed to a polar climate and their mountain chains, which constitute the spine of the islands, remain buried under snow all year round. It is not by chance that the name Svalbard means "cold coast."

374
Snow-covered mountains and frozen seas. This is the magnificent view of the Svalbard islands for the greater part of the year.

375
A glacier scarred by crevices (to the right) meets the frozen sea; we are on the island of Spitsbergen, in the Svalbard archipelago.

376-377
All the islands of the Svalbard archipelago are mountainous, but
the highest peaks rise on the
main island of Spitsbergen. The
highest of all, rising 5618 ft (1713
m) above sea level, is Newton-
toppen, located in the northeast
of the island.

A JOURNEY WHERE NATURE IS AT ITS MOST EXTREME

FLYING HIGH

FLYING HIGH NORWAY

379
A view over Troms, the county of which Tromsø (left)
is the capital. Every shade of green can be seen in this
wood near Tønsberg (right).

Only 4 percent of the 202,376 sq. miles (323,802 sq. km) of Norwegian territory has been urbanized or cultivated. For the most part, the most populous areas are to be found along the coasts and at the heads of the fjords. The rest of the country is made up of mountains and uplands, a wild and untamable landscape, populated by reindeer and arctic foxes, where the winds blow so fiercely that no tree can take root. Norway is long and narrow, widening at its southern end. Its shape is very much like a lute. In this territory there are two great plateaus: the Finnmark in the far north and the Hardangervidda on the opposite side, in the south. The latter is the most extensive plateau (*vidda*, in Norwegian) of the entire European continent, taking in more than 6200 sq. miles (10,000 sq. km) from east to west, from sea to sea, from Oslo to Bergen. We are at an altitude of approximately 4000-4250 ft (1200-1300 m) above sea level; the extreme western borders of the Hardangervidda are

considerably steep; the combined actions of the ancient glaciers and the numerous rivers formed by the melting snows have carved out the rock, thus creating the fjords and reshaping the mountains that plunge into the deep blue depths of the waters. It is in this landscape that man has achieved one of the most astonishing feats of railway engineering: the Flåm-Myrdal route the steepest standard-gauge, no-rack railway in the world. Within only 12 miles (20 km) it rises from sea level, from the bottom of the Aurlandfjord, to the 2811 ft (857 m) of the station at Myrdal, where it connects with the Oslo-Bergen line. The station seems to float in a deserted, ghostlike landscape of rocks and lichen, covered as it is with snow for at least five months out of the year. But in reality the station is a bustling intersection because here the tourists change trains to take the excursion known as "Norway in a Nutshell," a trip that takes in a stretch of the line where the train stops for a photo

380
The winters are extremely severe and the snowfalls heavy in
the hinterland of Narvik.

A Journey Where Nature
is at its Most Extreme

opportunity at the Kjosfossen waterfalls before going on to make the connection at Flåm, from where the boat follows the coast to leeward the Sognefjord and finally reaches Bergen. During the brief lasting summer, the thaw feeds thousands of streams, small lakes and marshes, flooding the highlands and cascading down into the valley in high waterfalls. Norwegians have managed to exploit this abundance of water to produce electricity. The Sima power plant is a giant built into the heart of the mountain. All systems, pipes and buildings are underground, so as not to cause any environmental impact. Just to give an idea of its capacity, every year almost 3 billion kWh are produced here in a totally clean manner. Despite the harsh conditions, many species of plants can be found on the Hardangervidda; their seeds have been carried great distances by the wind. Trees grow with great difficulty, bent as they are by the harsh winds; shrubs are thick and the terrain is forever covered with a soft, multicolored carpet of lichens and moss, the favorite food of the reindeer. It is precisely by following the reindeer paths that humankind reached the uplands some 7000 years ago; in the area of Haine, in fact, artifacts dating back to that era have been discovered. The paths which once were hunting tracks are now trodden by trekkers who, laden with their backpacks and all their equipment, follow these trails, staying over at refuges that are always open and where water and food are always available. Over a third of the Hardangervidda is now a National Park. Finnmark occupies the extreme tip of Norwegian territory before it reaches the perennial Arctic ice. This is the realm of the Sami or "Lapps," as they are known; it is a term used by Norwegians and Swedish alike, and not without a hint of racism. Proceeding north, the vegetation becomes ever lower and sparser, until it disappears altogether giving way to moss and lichens. Unlike the Hardangervidda, the Finnmarkvidda is somewhat lower, being nearer sea level, and less steep; to the east, it extends over to Sweden and eventually Finland. The internal areas are practically deserted and there are only two inhabited settlements of any size or significance: Kautokeino, with a population of about 2000, noted for reindeer breeding

A Journey Where Nature is at its Most Extreme

but totally devoid of any other appeal; and then Karasjok, the capital of the Sami people, where their parliament, the Folketinget, meets along and where the Sápmi, a very interesting cultural center/museum, has being created. Karasjok is also famous for the manufacturing of silver products. In the remaining areas of the *vidda*, there are only a few *siida*, the characteristic temporary villages with their *lavvu*, the Lapp tents made of reindeer skin which are surprisingly warm and comfortable and resistant to wind and water. The Sami people light a fire in the center of the tent to heat the interior and create a column of hot air that blocks out both rain and cold. These *siida* owe their origin to the fact that they were located at the intersections of the reindeer migratory paths, from inland to the coast in the fall and in the opposite direction in spring. Here, the Sami have been meeting annually for centuries to exchange news, trade goods and even arrange their weddings. Since 1989, they have enjoyed a large degree of autonomy with their own parliament, but only a few years ago these short, dark-skinned people of Asian descent with their almost almond-like eyes were not particularly well liked by more thoroughbred Norwegians. Mostly of Germanic stock, they considered the Sami to be merely good-for-nothing drunkards. Things have now changed, and today the Finnmark region is enjoying a revival of the Sami language and of its culture; a newspaper has been founded and primary and secondary schools opened. The language is particularly important since it constitutes the identifying factor between a non-Sami and a Sami; the latter registering themselves on a special list and so acquiring the right to vote for the Folketinget. One might ask what drives so many people to visit these inhospitable and isolated territories, following in the footsteps of Francesco Negri, the first "civilized" person in the 17th century to make his way on foot to the North Cape. Probably the great fascination of the *vidda* provides the dream. The Great North is a mental frontier where, despite the technical means now available, humankind still has to confront a merciless environment. For all believers it personifies God the Creator himself, whereas for agnostics it is the end result of a

In the proximity of the Søndre Folgefonna glacier, located on the Hordalan peninsula, the land is a lacework of small lakes and fjords.

long, evolutionary process. For everyone it has something of the superhuman, something that goes beyond and is greater than ourselves. The Finnmark region brings pure emotion; an imaginary symbol of the fight for survival against a prevailing nature. Darkness and extreme cold in winter, continuous light during its brief summer: these few words contain the essence of this part of Scandinavia, bounded by the Arctic Circle. In the inland part of Norway to the southwest begins the Oppland area, the mountainous internal district starting at the head of the Oslofjord, extending on toward the border with Sweden and ending up in the Trøndelag region, where Norway begins to narrow down to a mere strip of land squeezed between Sweden and the Norwegian Sea. The landscape here is very different from that of the vidda. Over there it was a bare and uninhabited upland plain, whereas here it is typically alpine, in character with towns of a certain importance. Among these is Eidsvoll, extremely important for the country since it was here that, on 17 May 1814, the first Norwegian constitution was drafted. Then there are Hamar, Gjøvik and also Lillehammer, famous for having hosted the 1994 Winter Olympics. Particularly in the south, the large valleys are widely cultivated and thick woodlands cover the mountains. The highest peaks of the country, the Glittertind, 8101 ft (2470 m), and the Galdhøpiggen, 8098 ft (2469 m), are to be found right here as well as Lake Mjøsa which, with its 142 sq. miles (368 sq. km), is Norway's largest lake. From the northern shore of lake Guldbrandsdalen, a valley 125 miles (200 km) long opens out to the north, following the course of the River Lågen until it reaches the inaccessible Rondane mountains and the Dovrefjell upland, with its rock formations and interweaving trees that resemble fantastic figures; these are the same figures that turn up in the numerous legends and tales of trolls, giants and fairies. The whole Rondane area, which extends for over 36 sq. miles (50 sq. km), forms a breathtaking landscape, as does Lake Gjerde at over 3000 ft (1000 m), lying alongside Sjoa and protected since 1962 by its status as a National Park, the first to be set up in the country. The Rondane area is the central feature of Norway's interior: vast plateaus, valleys

387

The green of the vegetation and the dark blue of the waters: these
are the typical colors of the southern part of Norway, near Oslo.

and the immense Ronde mountains that seal off the southern part of the area. Here are to be found 10 peaks over 6500 ft (2000 m), a record height for Scandinavia. To the north, the Rondane links up with the Dovre plateau, where Snøhetta, one of Norway's most famous mountains for its trekking and cross-country skiing facilities, stands out. In Otta the road divides: to the southeast, toward the Sognefjord, one comes to an area of glaciers along with the highest peaks of the country, up in the Jotunheimen National Park. This is considered one of the most spectacular areas of Norway, with its massive rocks, ravines, snow-capped peaks and glaciers. It therefore comes as no surprise that Jotun, in the Old Norse mythology, was the name of a giant and not particularly benign troll, and that heim comes from "home." The overall impression left by this environment, with its imposing, wild and often scary landscape, has heavily influenced the imagination of the ancient Nordic peoples, prompting them to create trolls, *nisser, hulder, nøkker* . . . evil creatures that populate woods, mountains and waterways and personify all the dangers and hardships of life amid such an imposing natural environment. To the northeast, the road reaches Ålesund. At Dombås it divides again and climbs north, toward Trondheim, crossing the uplands of Dovrefjell, an area particularly well-supplied with water with its many rivers and small lakes, among which the famous Lesjaskogvattnet. Parallel to the Guldbrandsdalen, farther to the west near the Swedish border and set apart from Rondane, the valley of the River Gläma rises toward the source of the river along the Swedish border.

Notwithstanding the mountainous environment, there are numerous populated settlements in the central valleys of Norway which have found tourism to be a notable contribution to economic well-being. Mention has already been made of Lillehammer, which become famous worldwide for its Winter Olympics; other areas are better known only locally because they have earned a reputation not as ski-resorts but as the departure points for the most fantastic excursions that go in search of enchanted worlds.

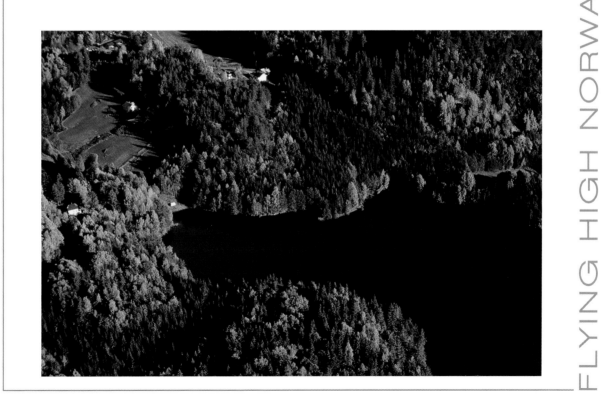

388-389
The low-lying lands around the Oslofjorden, in the vicinity of Norway's capital city, are covered by a large number of dense woods which come right down to the shoreline.

390-391
In the southern part of Norway, around the Oslofjorden, the country typically consists of gently undulating hills covered with pine woods.

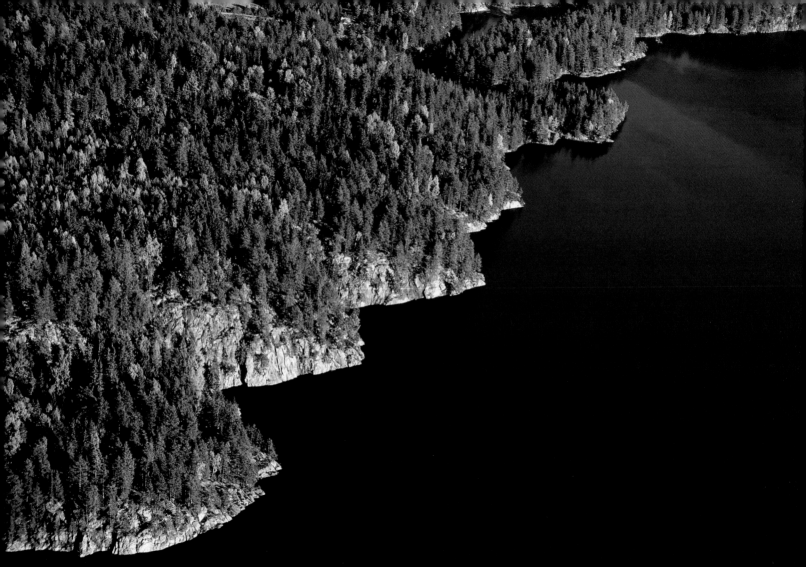

392 and 393
The pine woods lightly touch the waters of the Oslofjorden: we are not
very distant from the capital city, but the countryside is still hostile and
the inhabited settlements rare, lost in the woods.

394 and 395
The hinterland to the east of the capital, as far as the border with Sweden, is an alternation of water courses and flat or slightly undulating countryside; a fertile land favoured by a climate sufficiently mild to permit its cultivation.

396-397

A typical Norwegian farmstead peers out from the woodlands that encircle Oslo. Agriculture, for morphological and climactic reasons, is not widely practiced and represents only about 0.5 percent of the Norwegian gross national product.

398-399

Small lakes and woods are typical of the Buskerud county near Kongsberg, a municipality located in the south of the country, to the west of Oslo. The region is crossed by the Numedalslågen River, which flows into the sea farther to the south, at Larvik.

400 and 401
Norway is certainly not lacking in timber as a raw material. These photographs show a stockpile center near Tønsberg. These trunks are still transported on huge barges along the waterways; clearly an economical means of shifting vast quantities of timber from the hinterland to the coast.

402-403
Cultivated land seized from the forest gains way in the heart of the Tønsberg region in the Vestfold county, down in the south-east of Norway.

404 and 405
Extensive blankets of forest envelop the city of Tønsberg. The entire
county of Vestfold is rich in woodland – principally birch and pine –
spreading across the hinterland as far as the Skagerrak, the stretch of
sea that separates Norway from Denmark.

406 and 407
The deer is the king of the birch woods that lie along the Numedal-slågen River, near Larvik. This southern area of Norway is a sort of natural park where, side by side, cultivated land coexists with almost primitive woodland.

408
This photograph captures the essence of southern Norway: water, woods and fields. A boat moored in the river demonstrates the presence of man in this corner of Vestfold.

409 left
Woods and cultivated fields near Larvik bring to mind an abstract painting. As much as 23.1 percent of all Norwegian territory is covered by productive forests, whereas only a very small percentage is set aside for agriculture.

409 right
The warm colors of the late summer contrast with the whiteness of this small church near Larvik, in southern Norway.

410 and 411
A land of violent and unexpected contrasts, Norway continually offers romantic and striking glimpses of nature. These pictures depict the most mountainous area of the Vestfold county near Kragerø.

412 and 413
Life expectation in Norway is very close to 80 and is amongst the highest in the world; all the social indicators are positive and the quality of life is extremely high. The remarkable aspect is that Norway is not among the most industrialized of nations; Norwegian prosperity results from immense natural resources and from visitor-attracting landscapes, clearly visible in these pictures of southern regions of Vestfold.

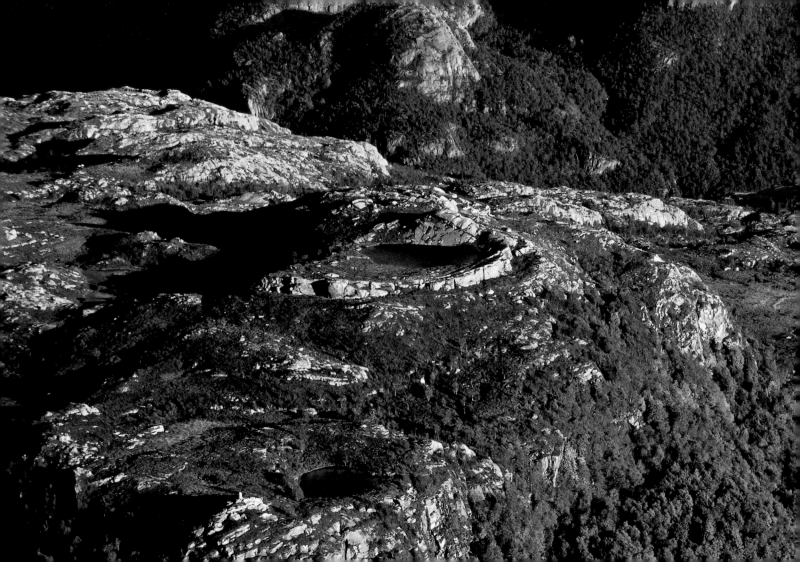

414-415
The hinterland of Rogaland, in the area between Stavanger and Eigersund, reflects the morphological structure of this part of Norway: it is crossed by fjords sometimes 125 miles (200 km) deep.

416-417
These sharply pointed peaks form real and valid natural frontiers separating the numerous fjords of the hinterland in the area between Stavanger and Eigersund.

418 and 419
In the foreground the fjords widen out like lakes, hemmed in by dense coniferous forests; in the distance the coastline splinters into a thousand islands. This is just one of many possible landscapes to be found in Rogaland, one of the most beautiful regions in the world.

420-421

A scene of primeval beauty, this sunset over the inland areas of Rogaland stirs up indescribable emotions: a flight over this region means flying over what is perhaps the most primitive and unspoiled area left on our planet.

422 and 423
The dams on the Telemark Canal intrude into a landscape of just small lakes and woodlands. The canal is the only waterway that links the interior of the country with the sea. There is an overall rise of some 236 ft (72 m) from the sea to Lake Flåvatn, from where one can continue on, still by water, as far as Dalen, about 100 miles (150 km) farther inland amongst the mountains of southern Norway.

424 and 425
Fertile countryside stretches inland from the coast between Bergen
and Rubbestadneset in the westernmost part of Norway.

426 and 427

The blue waters of these small lakes, which bring to mind similar ones in the Alps, peep out among the highlands of Hordaland. The county of Hordaland is in the mid-western part of the country and is split by the long and deep Hardangerfjorden. The territory of the Hordaland contains the greater part of the national park of Hardangervidda.

428-429

The county of Telemark is in the southeastern part of Norway and extends from the Hardangervidda plateau down to the coast. The countryside is a fascinating succession of wooded hills and valleys, crossed by the canal of the same name which divides the county lengthwise.

430-431
The action of the glaciers that covered this part of the Hordaland thousands of years ago is still evident in the shape of the hollowed-out valleys and in the crumpled "skin" of the mountain.

432 and 433
The Folgefonna National Park is of particular interest from a scientific angle as well as absolutely beautiful from a landscape viewpoint. By studying the morphology of the rocks found there, it has been possible to reconstruct the geological history of the period dating from 12,000 to 4000 BC.

434
This picture also clearly shows the traces left by the passing of the Folgefonna glacier in prehistoric times.

435
The shadow of the helicopter on the rounded mountains of the Folgefonna testifies to the hedge-hopping maneuvers carried out to better capture the beauty of a landscape that, not by chance, is protected by its status of nature reserve.

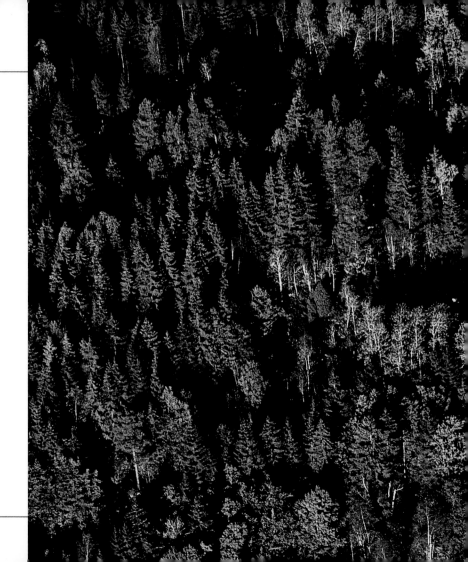

436-437
Sandefjord is on the south coast. The name in Norwegian means 'sandy fjord,' a well-deserved name judging by the foreground of this photograph. The fjord on which the city lies carries the un-pronounceable name of Sandefjordsfjorden.

438 and 439
Sandefjordsfjorden is a fjord about 6.5 miles (9 km) long in the county of Vestfold. It is located between the two peninsulas of Osteroya and Vesterøya. In this part of Norway the coast is low-lying and the terrain inland extremely fertile.

440 and 441
Extending inland, the Sande-fjordsfjorden is bordered by fertile ground won by battling with the woods, and run by small family enterprises whose identifying features are the farm buildings that can be seen in these pictures.

442 and 443
The inland area behind Narvik occupies the narrowest part of Norway. From the Otofjord on the border with Sweden to Riksgräns are just the 4 miles (6 km) of a stiff climb. In this narrow strip of approximately 125 miles (200 km) there are several mountain peaks approaching 5000 ft (1500 m) in height.

444 and 445
For the greater part of the year, snow covers the crests that look down over the fjords of Nordland in the Narvik hinterland. The temperatures here are more severe than on the coast since the peaks do not benefit from the warming effect of the sea, but the water never freezes over.

446 and 447
The mountains near Narvik, in Nordland, are barely over 3500 ft (1000 m). Even so, the abundant winter snowfalls create a veritable high-mountain landscape.

448

To the north of Narvik the mountains slope down gradually into upland plains, continually interspersed with small lakes. Behind the mountains in the background is the border with Sweden.

449

Just like the grass that breaks out of the snow in springtime, so the bare trees of this forest near Narvik reach out toward the sun, waiting for the warmer season.

450 and 451
The winter snows cover the Nordand hinterland with a thick blanket.
The houses and roads show that man is always present, even in such
apparently unwelcoming places.

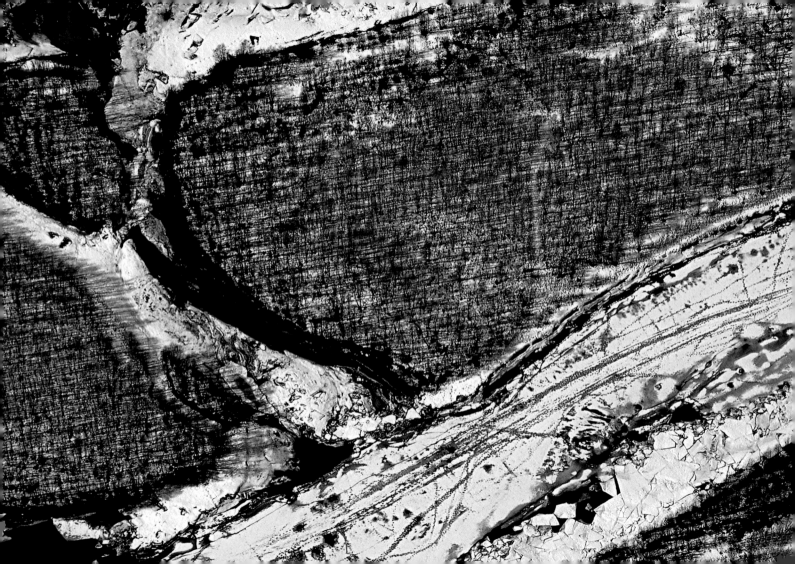

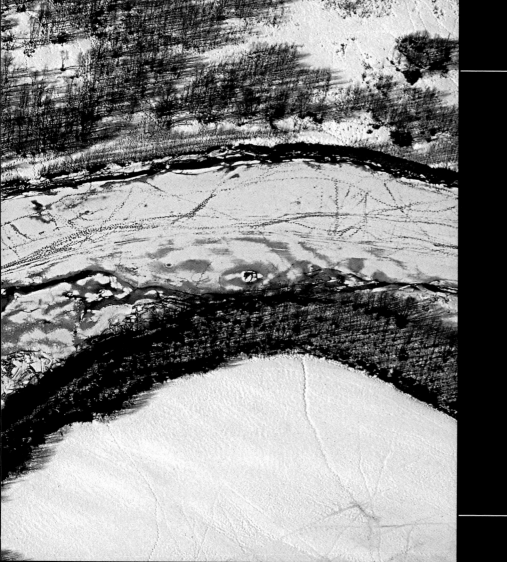

452-453

A river of snow and ice makes its way through a coniferous forest: this is the hinterland behind Narvik, toward the end of winter.

FLYING HIGH NORWAY

455
The wind drives the snow up against the trees, the snow melts where there are open spaces: the result is like an abstract painting which gives an idea of the impressions one gets when looking down over the Nordland countryside toward the end of winter.

456 and 457
At the latitude where Narvik is located, the high vegetation begins to diminish: the hardwood forests give way to the conifers and, as the Arctic Circle gets closer, even these disappear.

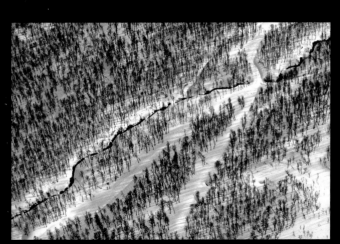

458 and 459
Like cracks in a sheet of glass, the torrents that form when the ice melts in springtime cut through the wooded cloak covering Nordland, behind Narvik.

460 and 461
In the inner regions of Troms, inside the Arctic Circle, the winter snowfalls are so intense and the climate so rigid that this white mantle maintains this impenetrable look well into the spring. The mountains in the background are a little over 3300 ft (1000 m), the peak being the Haltiatunturi, 4355 ft (1328 m) high, on the border with Finland.

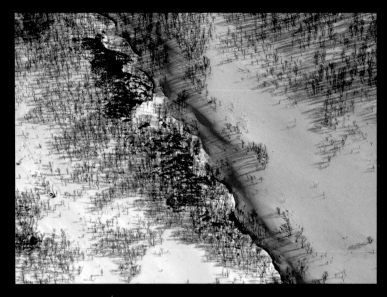

462 and 463
A stream in springtime,a winding lane lost in the countryside between woods and tiny settlements: all the rest in Troms is snow. This is the hinterland of Tromsø, where the winter lasts for six months.

464, 465 and 466-467
The woods in the county of Troms extend from the coast up to the border with Finland's Lapland. These pictures were taken at the end of winter near the Reisa National Park, a reserve that contains the wonderful Reisadal with its 882 ft (269 m) Mollis waterfall.

469

The county of Troms is predominantly mountainous and the latitude is such that the climate inland is decidedly severe. The land can only be used for breeding livestock. This photograph was taken at the narrowest point of the county, between Storfjord and the Swedish border: to the left can be seen the fjord of Larsbergbukta, and to the right the slopes of the mountain range.

470 and 471
The mountain ranges in the county of Troms are typically rounded: this is the result of thousands of years of activity by wind and ice which has gradually shaped the granite of which the mountains are composed in this part of Norway.

472 and 473

Troms is the county of mountains and water, even though its countryside for six months of the year reveals just the one color: white. In these photographs the bottom of a fjord can be seen, still frozen over and covered with snow at the beginning of springtime.

474-475
The water produced by the melting of the snow in spring runs
down the mostly mountainous
eastern part of Troms, where it
feeds the numberless sheets of
water and fjords scattered
throughout the region.

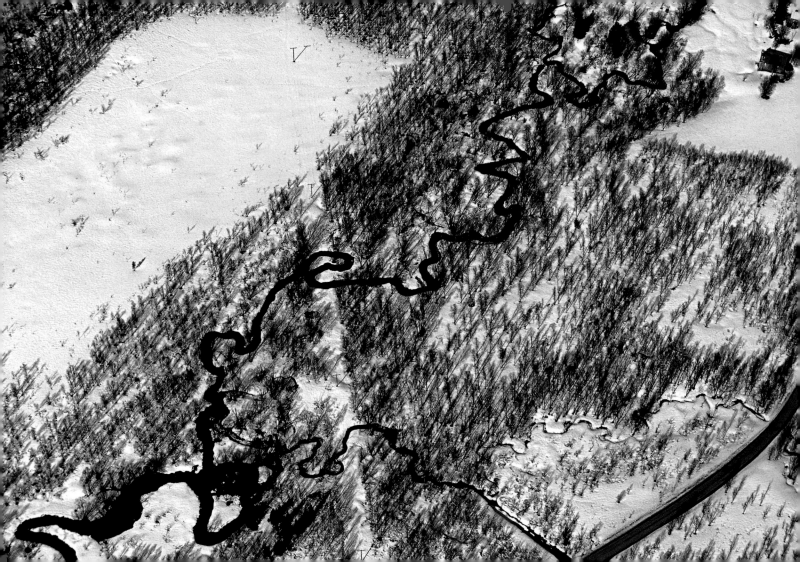

476 and 477
From rivers of ice to rivers of water: the winter freeze has scarcely relaxed its grip before the lowland areas of Troms become crossed by twisting, snakelike streams of water, which cut into the white blanket and create these genuine works of art.

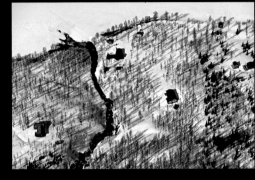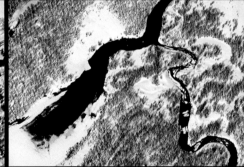

478-479

The production of fresh water in springtime along with the plentiful rainfalls at these latitudes explain the singular character of the Norwegian fjords. Even though they come into direct contact with the sea, they have a low saline content and have currents continually running through them: on the surface the water is warmer and saltier, deeper down it becomes colder and more fresh.

480-481

Finnmark is the northernmost county of Norway. The countryside one encounters is primeval, such as this valley near the course of the Tana River, dominated by forests and glacial lakes.

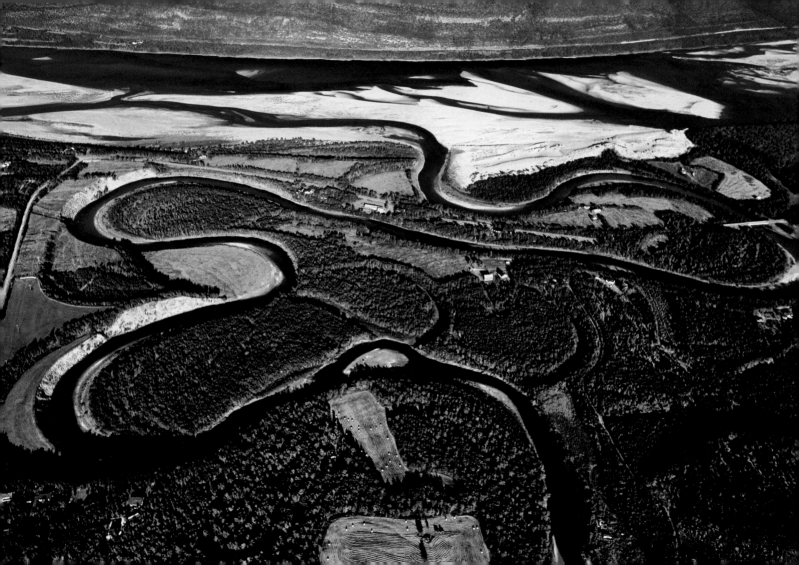

482
The Tana River, in the Finnmark region at the extreme north of Norway, is noted for the abundance of fish in its waters: here a record-breaking salmon was caught that weighed 77 lbs (35 kg).

483
The River Tana, also known as the Tanaelv, is 205 miles (330 km) long and crosses a territory that is for the most part flat. The route it takes, which mainly marks the border between Norway and Finland, is therefore slow and meandering.

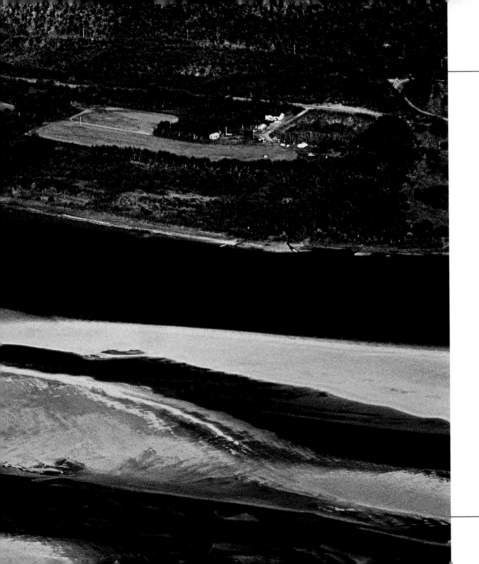

484-485
Before flowing into the Tanafjorden, the Tanaelv crosses the Finnmark, shaping the landscape and carrying along with it masses of sediment. Along its course, it slides by fields and forests before passing the city of Tana, where every year salmon fishermen gather from all over the world.

486 and 487
Large islands of sand, produced by the flows of the icy waters, rub up against the forests and pastures of Finnmark, along the course of the Tana River. Already known to, and frequented by, fishermen from all over the world, this region has also begun to attract significant numbers of tourists, thanks to the rich attractiveness of its countryside.

488 and 489

The Tana River, along with the North Cape, is possibly the most precious pearl, touristically speaking, of the Finnmark region. The county, which has Hammerfest as its capital, is the most extensive in Norway but the least populated.

490-491

Finnmark in summer offers landscapes of extraordinary beauty, which are highly appreciated by visitors from Finland who feel very much at home here. Tourism, however, is not yet a decisive factor in the development of the county: the local economy, for the most part, relies on the exploitation of its timber forests and mining resources, as well as on its fishing industry.

492-493
The land well beyond the Arctic Circle, in the northern part of Finnmark, is subject to permafrost and therefore remains permanently frozen. In reality the surface layer, which can extend from just a few inches to several feet in depth, melts during the summer (creating the wonderfully playful water effects shown here) only to freeze again in the winter; only the lowest layer remains permanently frozen.

494 and 495
The pictures show the magnificent countryside around the inland areas of the Tanafjorden. It is the Hvidda, the rocky plateau of Finnmark near the border with Finland and, a little farther on, with Russia. Its appearance is barren and inhospitable and not surprisingly so, since in an area a quarter the size of Italy there are only 80,000 inhabitants.

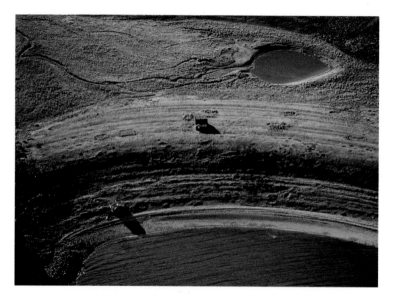

496 and 497
Glacial lakes both large and small are to be found all over the southern part of Finnmark, a very striking territory where the occasional
conifer forests willingly leave space for the great pasturelands much
loved by the reindeer and caribou. This is the Norwegian part of Lapland, where it is estimated that the Lapp population has been settled
for at least 2000 years.

498-499

Finnmark forms part of Lapland, which extends into four countries: Norway, Sweden, Finland and Russia's Baltic north. In this widespread territory, free of ice for only five months of the year, live many Sami, of whom there are 40,000 in northern Norway. The Sami are still very much attached to their traditions and claim possession of the land and its grazing rights for their reindeer-breeding activities.

Index

Index

Index

GRAZIANO CAPPONAGO DEL MONTE, WAS BORN IN MILAN IN 1959. AFTER COMPLETING HIS DEGREE IN SCANDINAVIAN LANGUAGES, HE CHOSE EUROPE, PARTICULARLY THE GERMANIC AND SCANDINAVIAN TERRITORIES, AS HIS IDEAL TRAVEL DESTINATIONS. SINCE 1983 CAPPONAGO DEL MONTE HAS MADE MANY VISITS TO DENMARK, NORWAY, SWEDEN AND FINLAND. HE RESIDED IN FINLAND FOR A LENGTHY PERIOD AND HAS RECORDED THE COUNTRY'S RICHES AND NATURAL BEAUTY IN NUMEROUS FEATURED ARTICLES. A PROFESSIONAL JOURNALIST AND PHOTOGRAPHY ENTHUSIAST, CAPPONAGO DEL MONTE WRITES FOR AND COLLABORATES WITH MANY TRAVEL AND VACATION MAGAZINES, FOCUSING ON THE NATURAL ENVIRONMENT AND LOCAL CUSTOMS AND CULTURES OF HIS DESTINATIONS.

Photo credits

All photographs are by Antonio Attini/Archivio White Star except the following:

pages 370 and 371 M. Watson/Ardea.com
page 372 Martin Roger/Getty Images
page 373 WireImageStock/Masterfile/Sie
pages 374, 375, 376-377 Doug Allan/Naturepl.com/Contrasto

The publisher would like to thank Ronnie Natvig (Kristiansand) and Andria (Lofoten).

© 2008 WHITE STAR S.P.A.
Via Candido Sassone, 22-24
13100 Vercelli - Italy
WWW.WHITESTAR.IT

TRANSLATION: MADDALENA NEALE

ISBN 978-88-544-0283-6

REPRINTS: 1 2 3 4 5 6   12 11 10 09 08

Color separation: Chiaroscuro and Fotomec, Turin
Printed in China

504

Rogaland frequently offers views
such as this one: small cottages
and boat sheds a few steps from
the sea.

FLYING HIGH